ORCHESTRA COMPANION

JAMES KJELLAND • **JACQUELYN DILLON**

Dear Students,

Strictly Strings Orchestra Companion is designed to help you develop both technique and musicianship. Rather than learning page-by-page as with Books 1 & 2, Book 3 is organized by key signature so you can use it more like an encyclopedia. It can be used in either large or small ensemble settings, or in private lessons. Each key signature has a four-page format:

1st page: ***Scales and Arpeggios***
2nd page: ***Bowing, Fingering, Shifting and Composition Studies***
3rd page: ***Etude, Duet and Chorale***
4th page: ***Orchestral Excerpts***

You can look up the key signatures at the top of each page, or use this page as a table of contents:

Best wishes in your continued musical adventures with *Strictly Strings Orchestra Companion!*
Sincerely,

James Kjelland

Jacquelyn Dillon

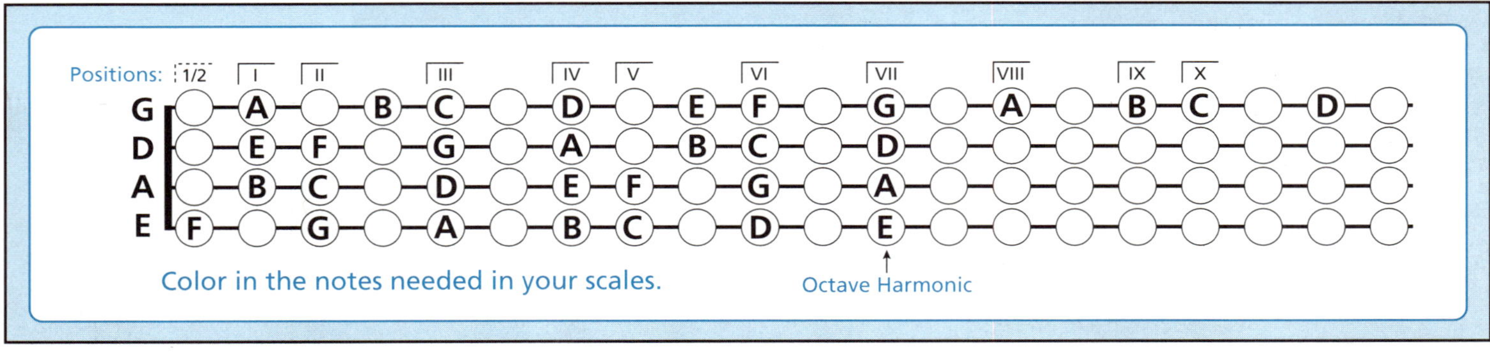

Mark in the half steps (∧)

C Major Scale

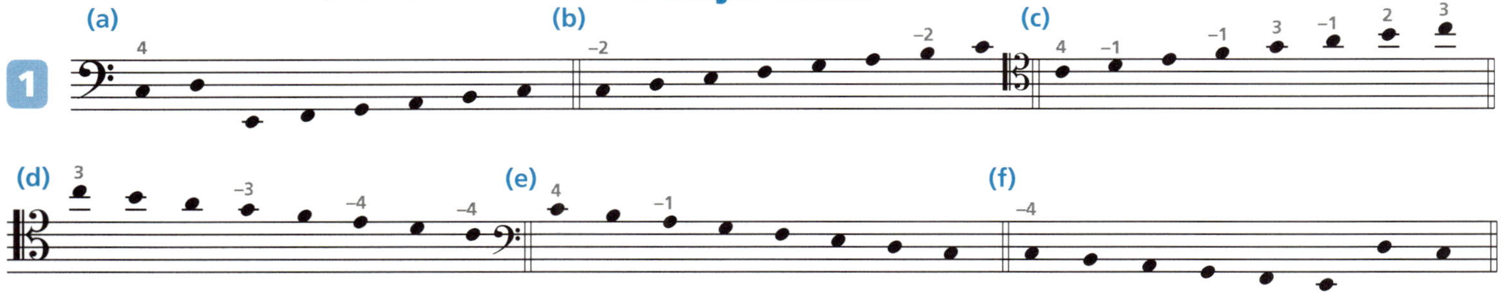

1 (a) (b) (c)

(d) (e) (f)

Scale in Thirds

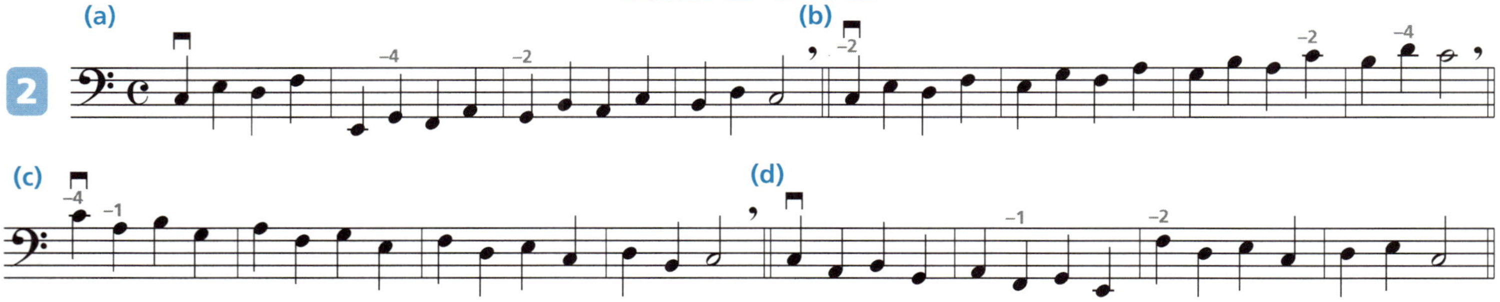

2 (a) (b)

(c) (d)

I Chord Arpeggio

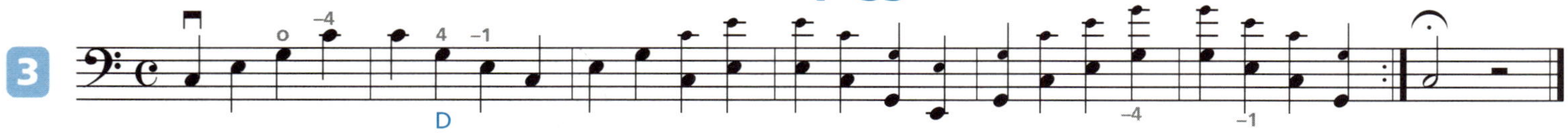

3

IV Chord Arpeggio V⁷ Chord Arpeggio

4

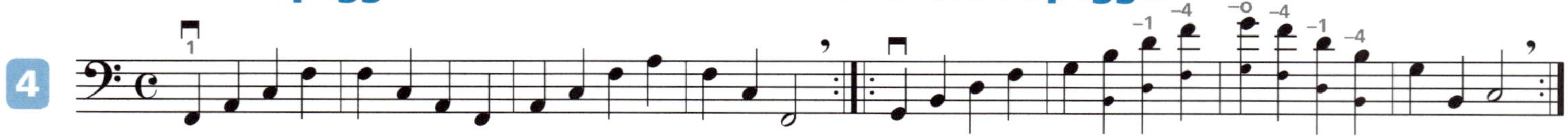

Mark in the half steps (∧)

A Harmonic Minor Scale

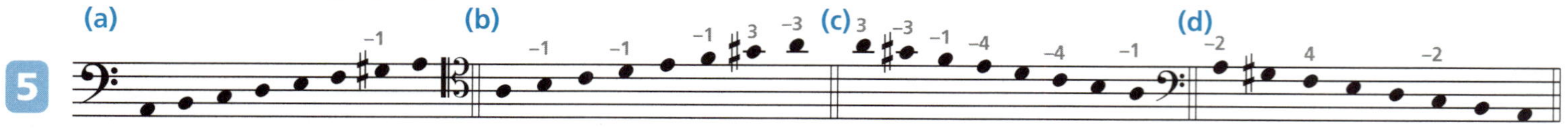

5 (a) (b) (c) (d)

i Chord Arpeggio

6

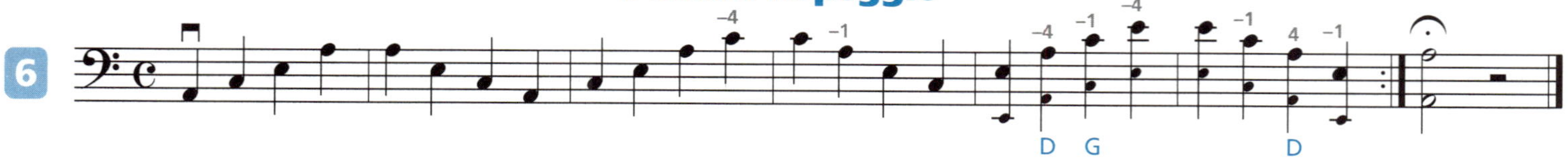

D G D

iv Chord Arpeggio V⁷ Chord Arpeggio

7

D D G

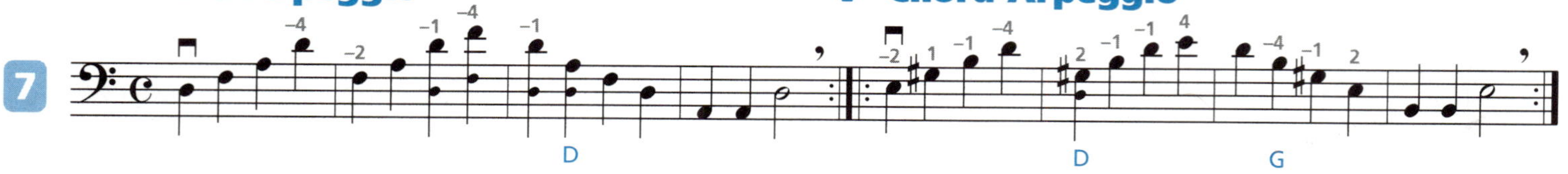

Bowing Theme

Based on J.S. Bach's
Little Fugue in G Minor

1
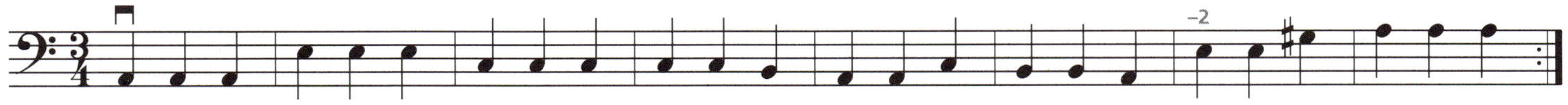
–2

Rhythm and Bowing Variations

2
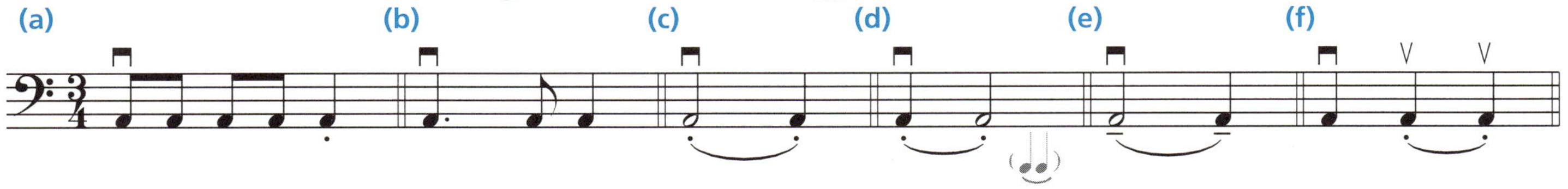
(a)
(b)
(c)
(d)
(e)
(f)

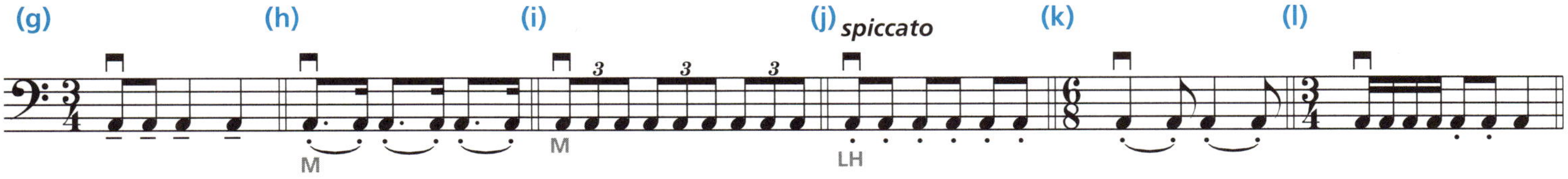
(g)
(h)
(i)
(j) spiccato
(k)
(l)
M
M
LH

Frère Jacques (Round)

(Fingering Theme)

French Folk Song

3
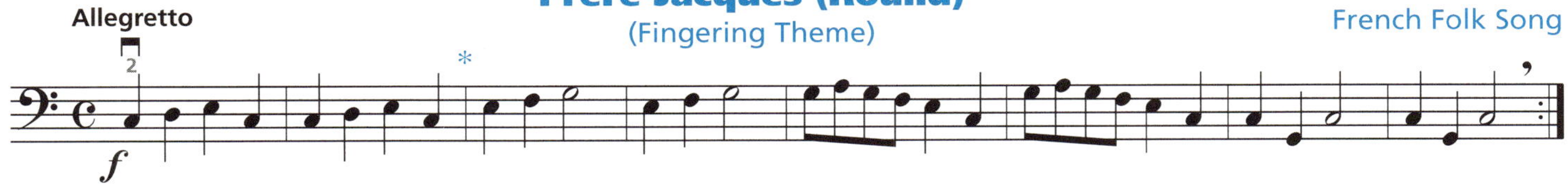
Allegretto
2
f

Variation I

4
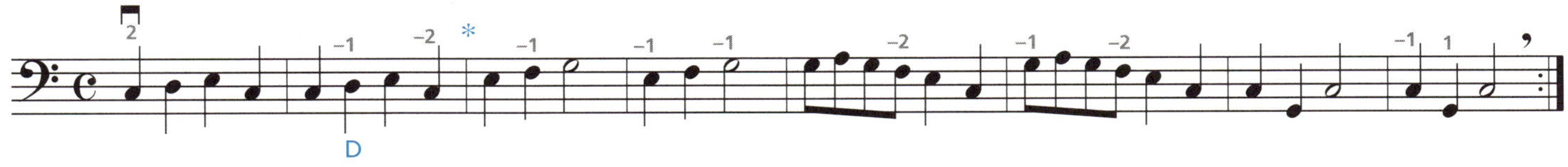
2
–1
–2
–1
–1
–1
–2
–1
–2
–1
1
D

Variation II

5
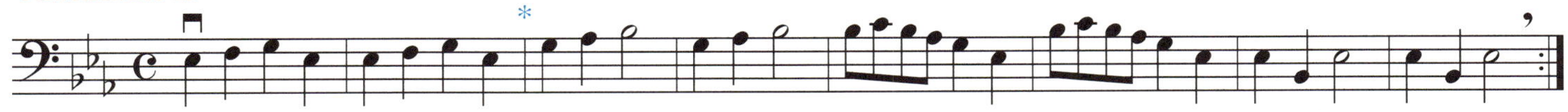

Shifting Patterns

Mark in the half steps (^)

6
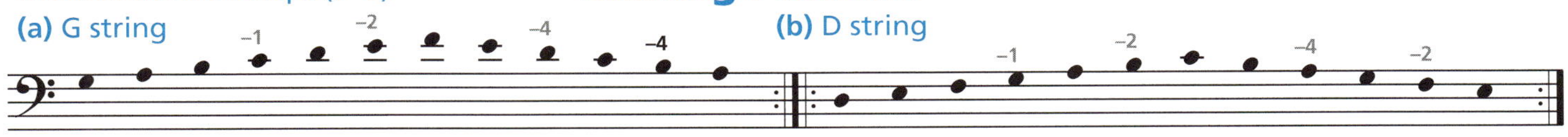
(a) G string
–1
–2
–4
–4
(b) D string
–1
–2
–4
–2

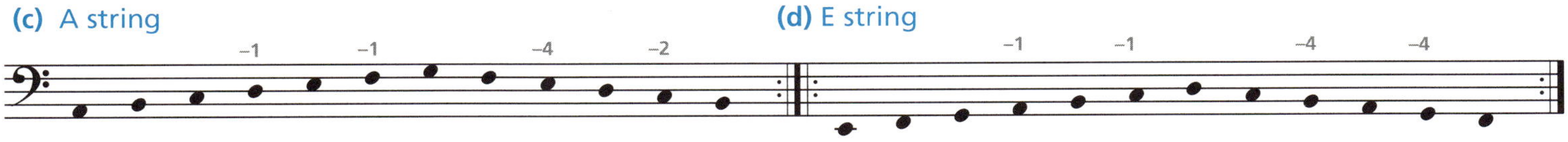
(c) A string
–1
–1
–4
–2
(d) E string
–1
–1
–4
–4

Rhythm and Bowing Variations

7
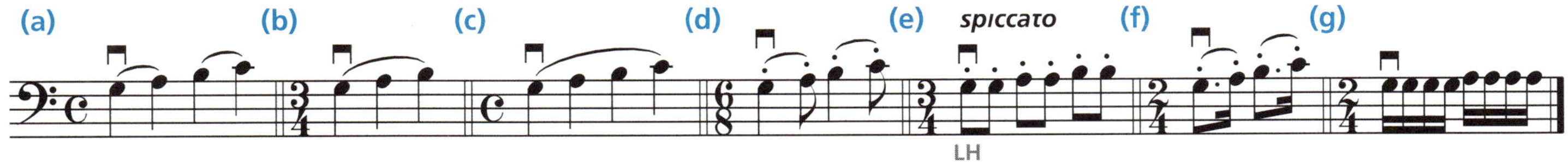
(a)
(b)
(c)
(d)
(e) spiccato
(f)
(g)
LH

Composition Corner
Make up a new rhythm

"Bile" Them Cabbage Down

American Folk Song

8
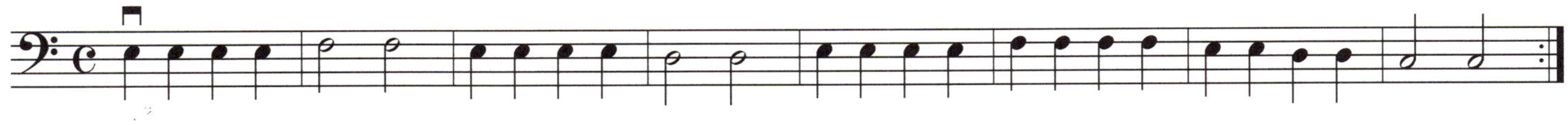

Etude
Op. 48, No. 2
Schröder
Allegretto
f
9
Farandole
(from L'Arlesienne Suite No. 2)
Bizet
Allegro
spiccato ♪'s
mp
simile
mf
A
B
spiccato ♪'s
mp
simile
f
13
f
ff
Goin' Home
(from the "New World" Symphony)
Dvořák
pp
mf
f
mp
rit.

March to the Scaffold
(from *Symphony Fantastique*)

Berlioz

Allegretto non troppo

Russian Sailor's Dance
(from *The Red Poppy*)

Glière

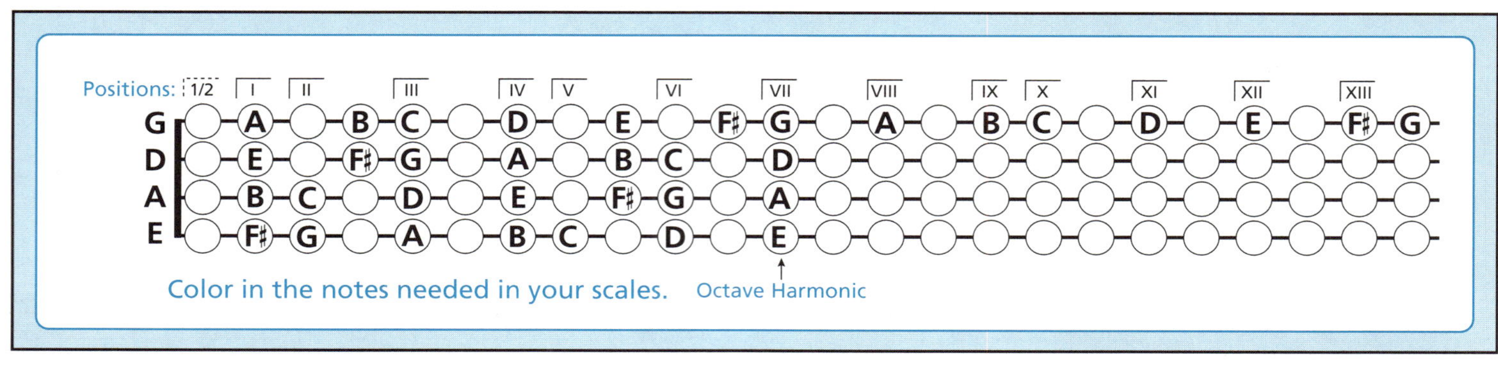

Mark in the half steps (∧)

G Major Scale

1 (a) (b) (c) (d) (e) (f)

Scale in Thirds

2 (a) (b) (c) (d)

I Chord Arpeggio

3

IV Chord Arpeggio   V⁷ Chord Arpeggio

4

Mark in the half steps (∧)

E Melodic Minor Scale

5 (a) (b) (c) (d)

i Chord Arpeggio

6

IV Chord Arpeggio   V⁷ Chord Arpeggio

7

Bowing Theme

from Grieg's *Holberg Suite*

1

Rhythm and Bowing Variations

2

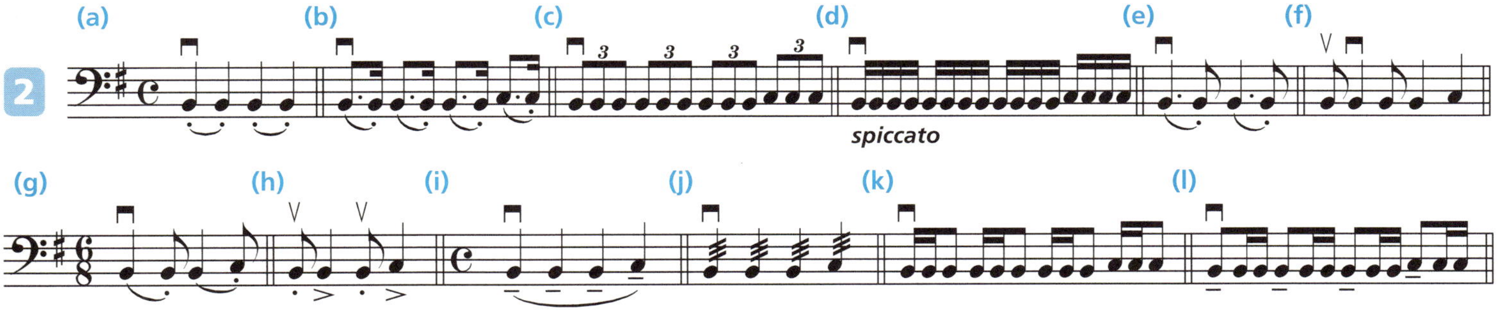

(a) (b) (c) (d) (e) (f)

spiccato

(g) (h) (i) (j) (k) (l)

Au Claire de la Lune
(Fingering Theme)

French Folk Song

3

Andantino   *Fine*   *D.C. al Fine*

mf-p   *f*   *mf*

Variation I

4

Fine   *D.C. al Fine*

D   *f*   *mf*

mf-p

Variation II

5

Fine   *D.C. al Fine*

mf-p   *f*   *mf*

Shifting Patterns

Mark in the half steps (⌢)

(a) G string   **(b)** D string

6

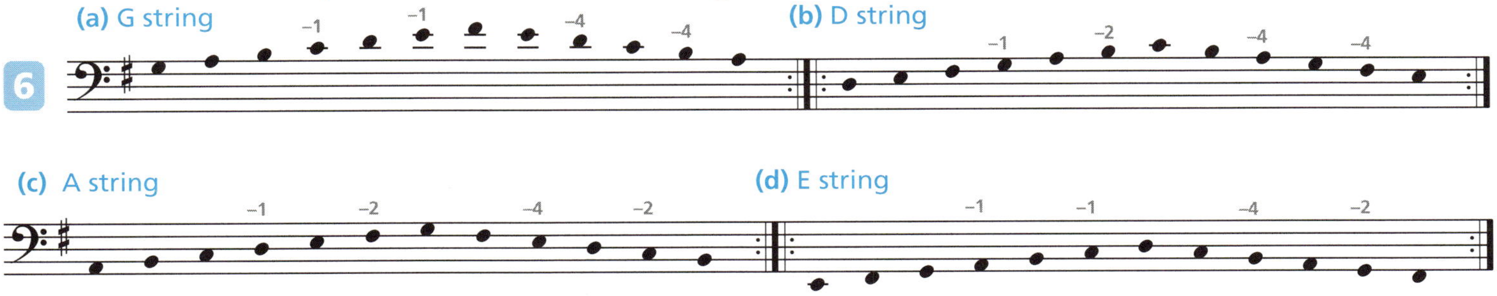

(c) A string   **(d)** E string

Rhythm and Bowing Variations

7

(a) (b) (c) (d) (e) *spiccato* (f) (g)

LH

Twinkle, Twinkle Little Star

Composition Corner

Play "by ear" starting on each of the following pitches

(a) (b) (c) (d)

8

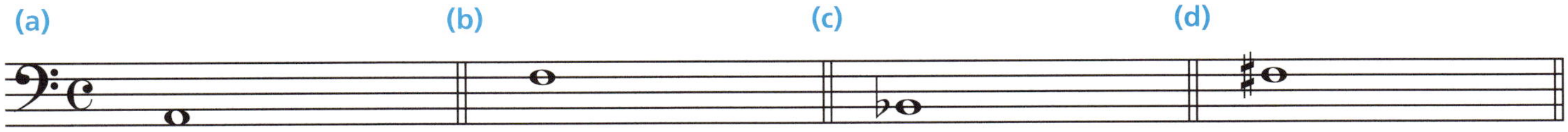

Etude

Dotzauer

Theme from Symphony No. 8 in G Major
(Third movement)

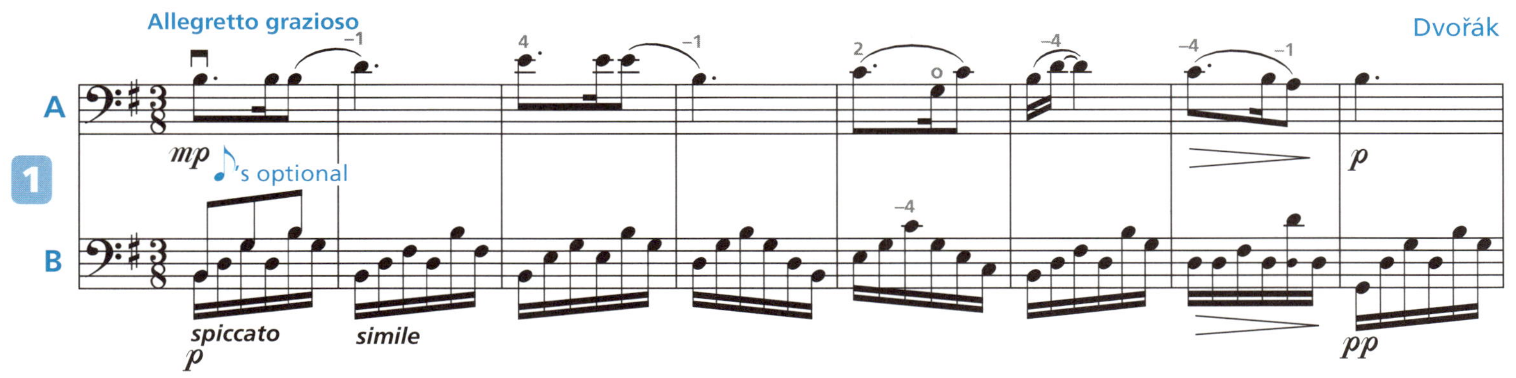

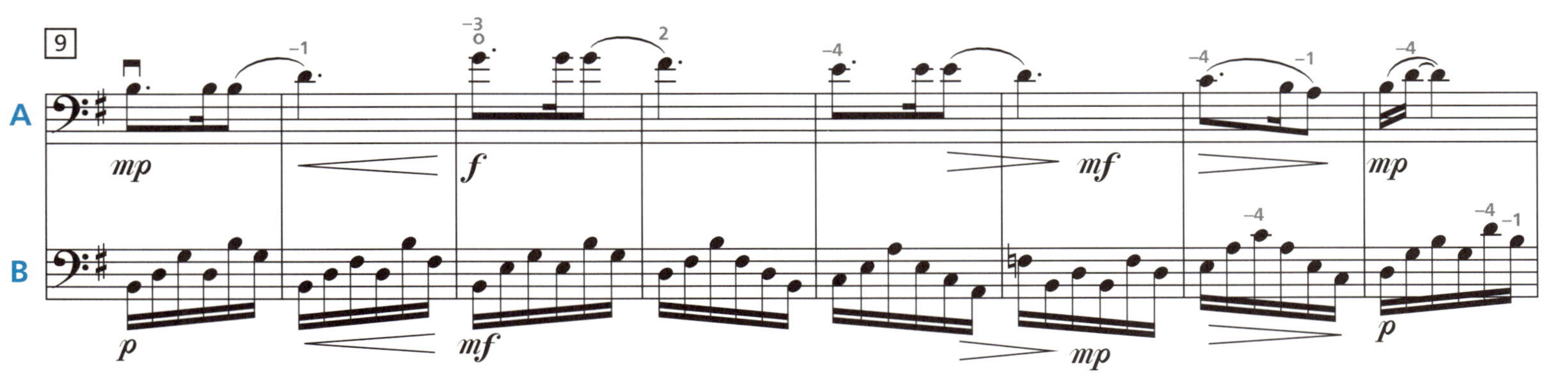

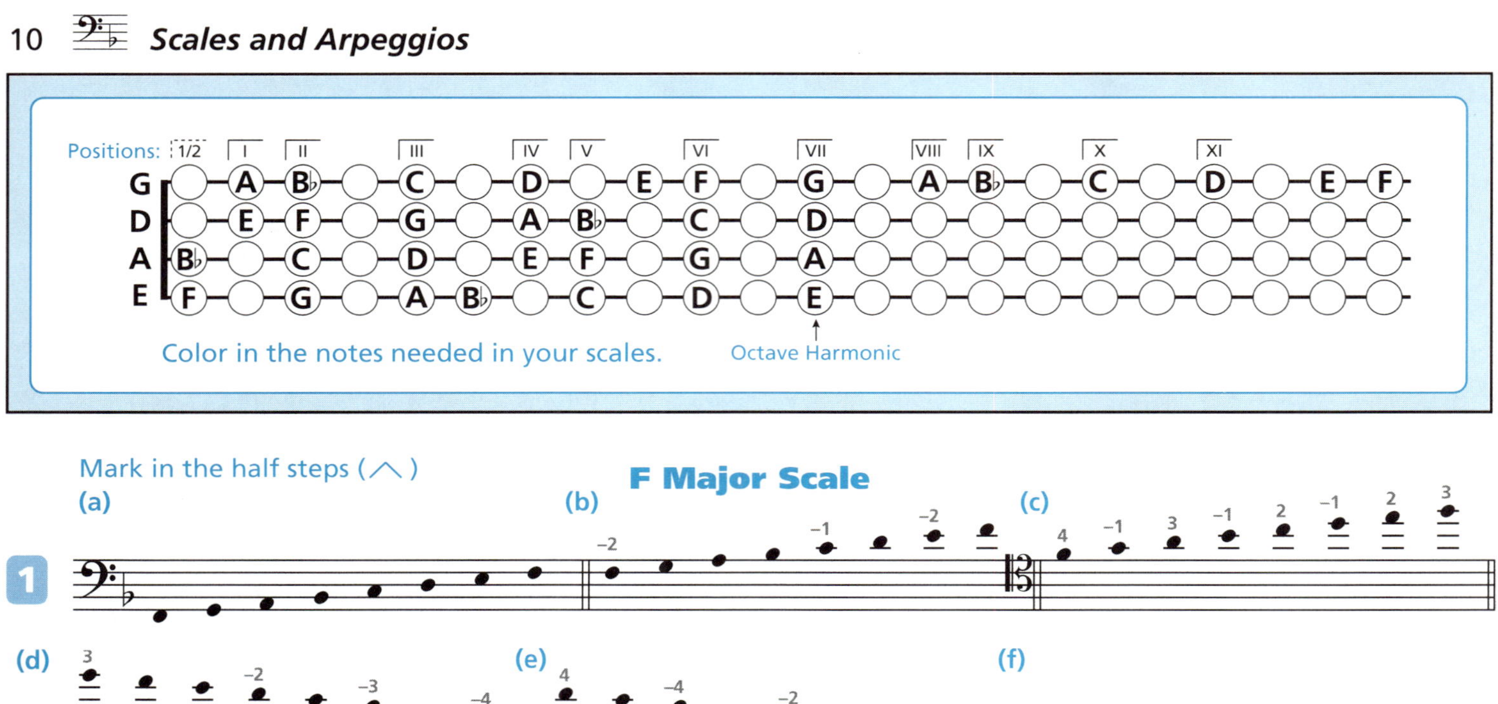

Mark in the half steps (⌃)

F Major Scale

(a) (b) (c)

1

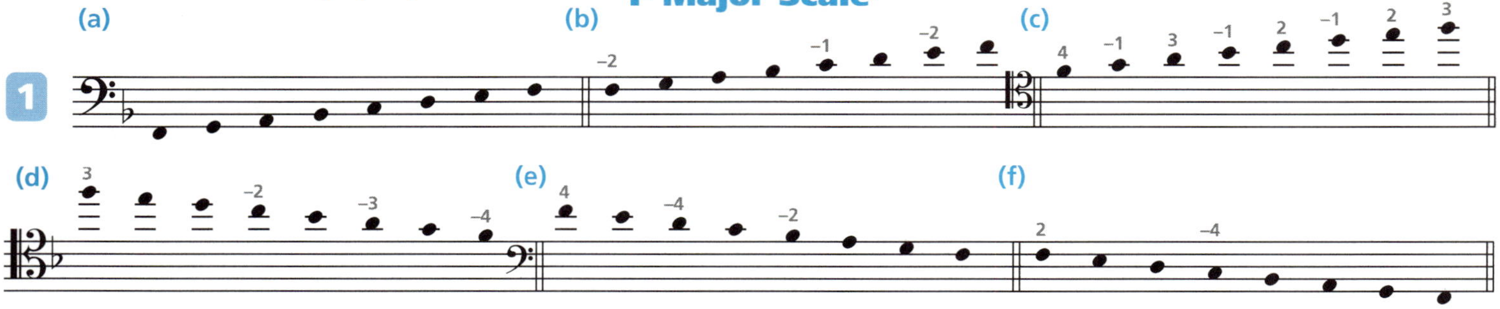

(d) (e) (f)

Scale in Thirds

(a) (b)

2

(c) (d)

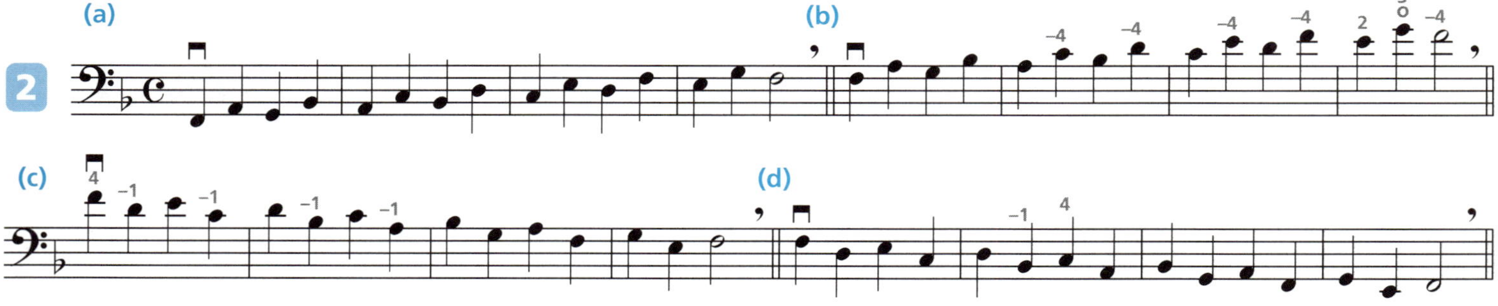

I Chord Arpeggio

3

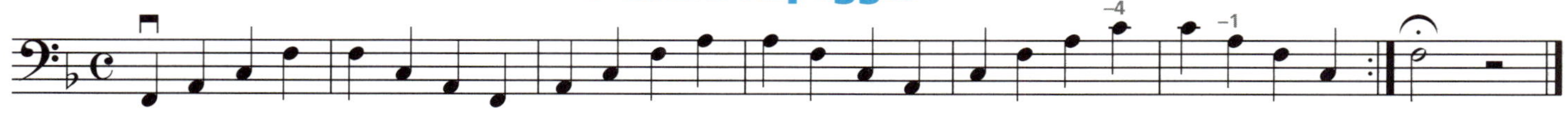

IV Chord Arpeggio

V⁷ Chord Arpeggio

4

Mark in the half steps (⌃)

D Harmonic Minor Scale

(a) (b) (c) (d)

5

i Chord Arpeggio

6

iv Chord Arpeggio

V⁷ Chord Arpeggio

7

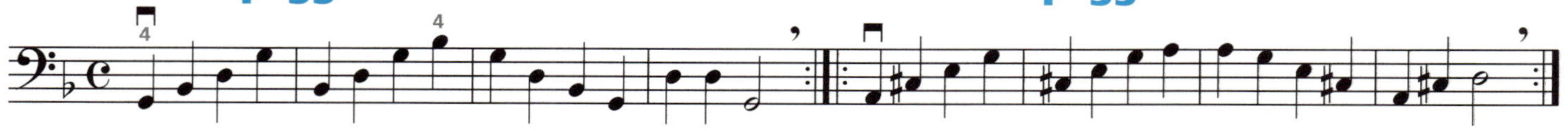

Bowing Theme

Irish Folk Tune

1

Rhythm and Bowing Variations

(a) **(b)** **(c)** **(d)** **(e)** **(f)**

2

etc. *3 3 3* *etc.*

(g) **(h)** **(i)** **(j)** **(k)** **(l)**

etc. *3 3*

Allegro

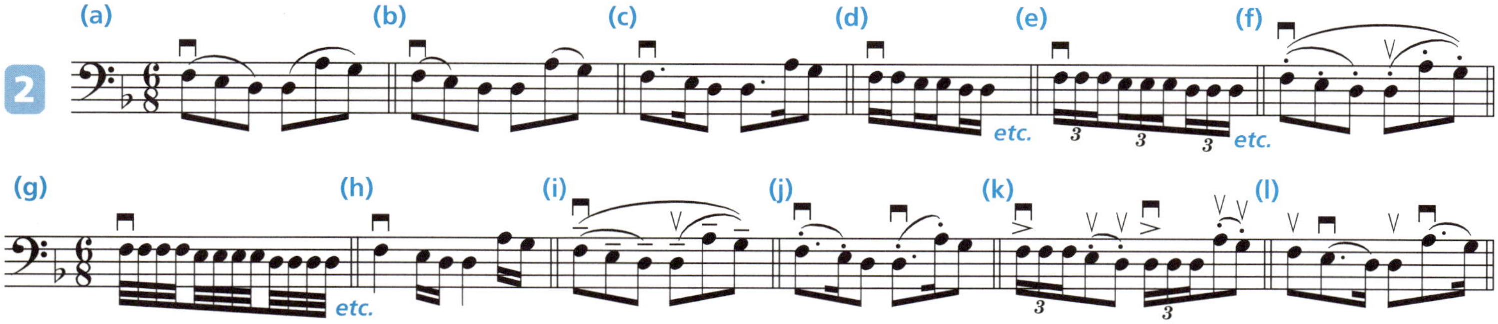

This Old Man
(Fingering Theme)

American Folk Song

3

mf *sim.* *f*

Variation I

4

mf D *sim.* *f* D

Variation II

5

mf *sim.* *f*

Mark in the half steps (⌃)

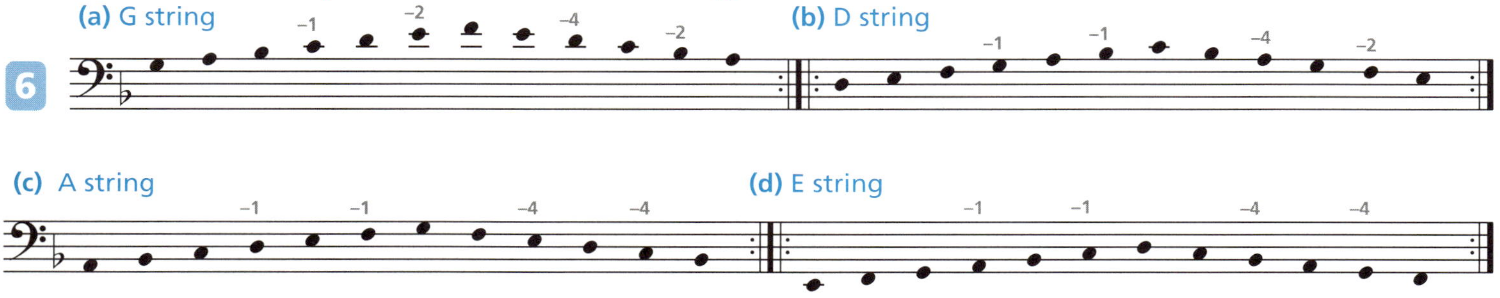

Shifting Patterns

(a) G string **(b)** D string

6

(c) A string **(d)** E string

Rhythm and Bowing Variations

(a) **(b)** **(c)** **(d)** **(e)** *spiccato* **(f)** **(g)**

7

WB WB WB M

Composition Corner
Compose and play a melody which includes these notes.

8

Double Stop Etude
(Op. 120, No. 7)
Dotzauer
Allegro moderato
mf
cresc.
15
f
f
ff
Invention in D Minor
J.S. Bach
Allegro
A
mf
D
B
mf
D
sim.
A
11
B
sim.
A
f
rit.
B
f
rit.
Ase's Death
(from Peer Gynt Suite, No. I)
Grieg
Andante doloroso
p
pp

Theme from Symphony No. 6

"The Pastorale"

Beethoven

Theme from Night on Bald Mountain

Mussorgsky

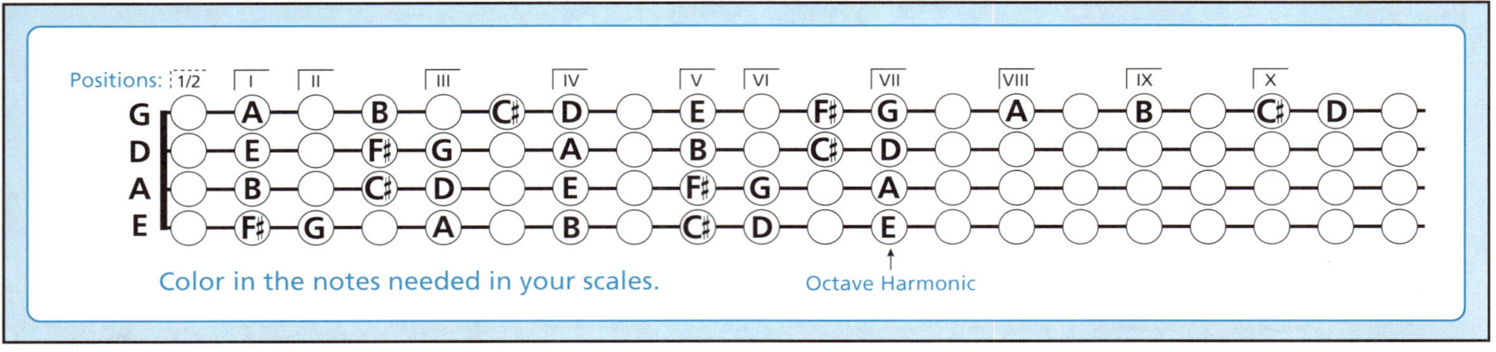

Mark in the half steps (∧)

D Major Scale

1. (a) (b) (c)
(d) (e) (f)

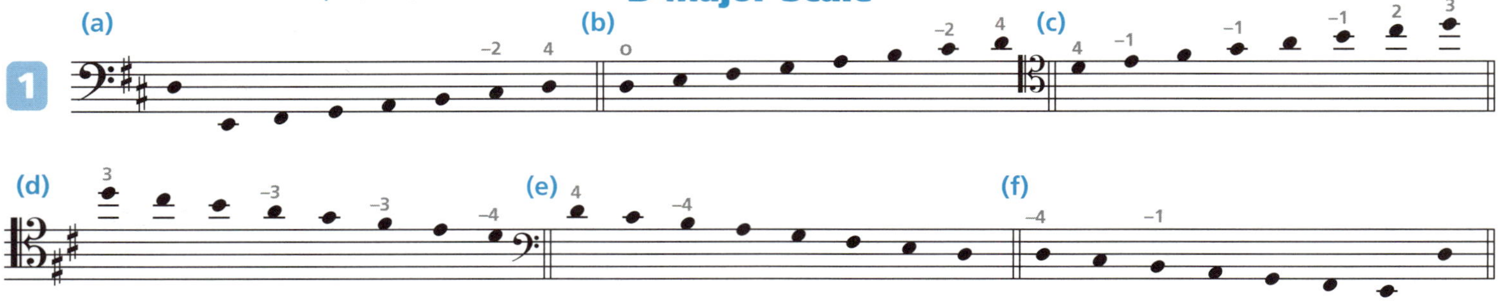

Scale in Thirds

2. (a) (b)
(c) (d)

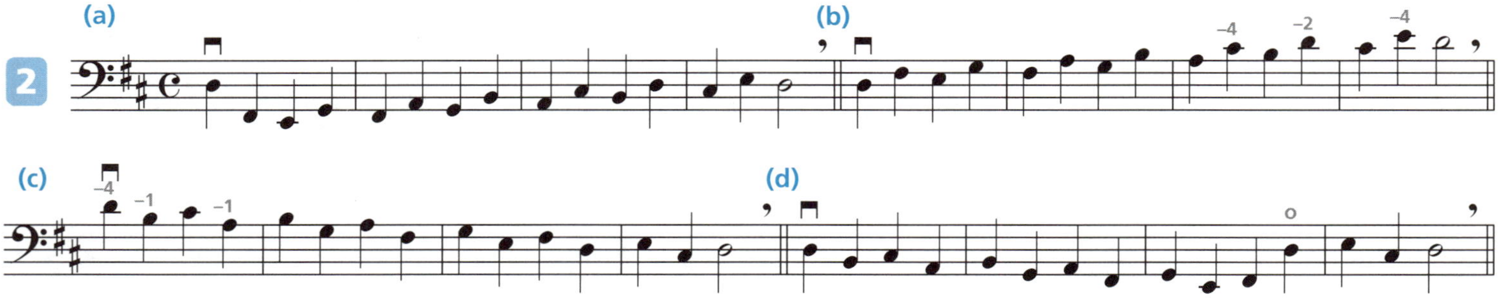

I Chord Arpeggio

3.

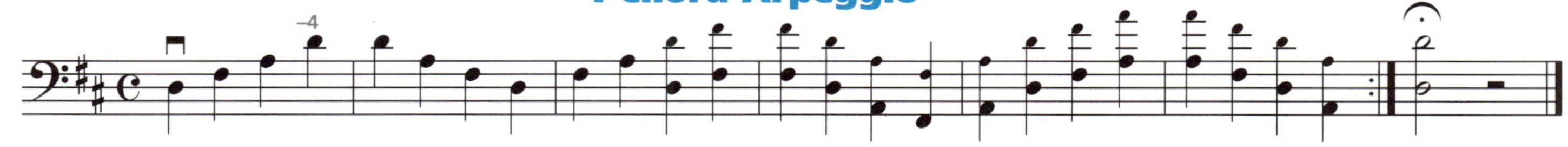

IV Chord Arpeggio

V⁷ Chord Arpeggio

4.

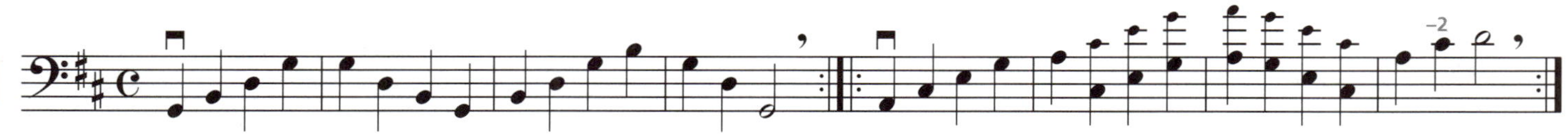

Mark in the half steps (∧)

B Melodic Minor Scale

5. (a) (b) (c) (d)

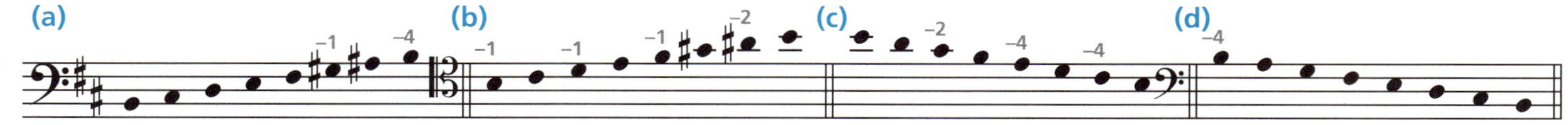

i Chord Arpeggio

6.

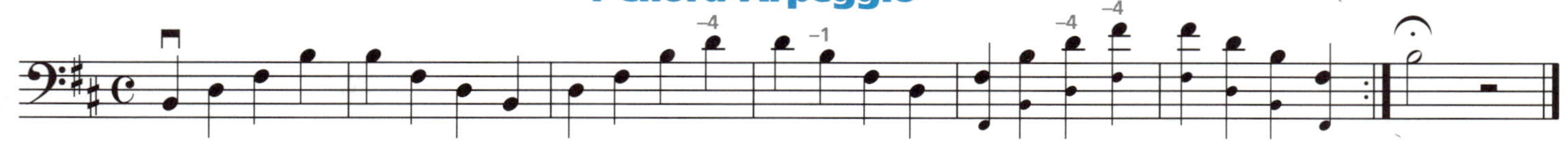

IV Chord Arpeggio

V⁷ Chord Arpeggio

7.

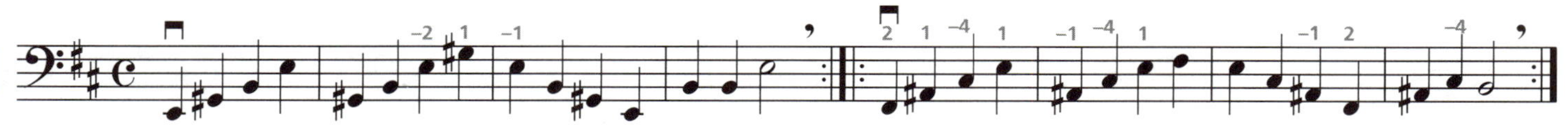

Bowing Theme
(Dies irae)
Rhythm and Bowing Variations
(a) (b) (c) (d) (e) (f)
UH
(g) (h) (i) (j) spiccato (k) (l)
M etc. Frog LH etc. UH
Theme from Violin Concerto in D Major
Allegro ma non troppo (Fingering Theme) Beethoven
mf
Variation I
mf D
Variation II
mf
Mark in the half steps
Shifting Patterns
(a) G string (b) D string
(c) A string (d) E string
Rhythm and Bowing Variations
(a) (b) (c) (d) (e) (f) (g) spiccato
etc.
Composition Corner
Write out and play the Beethoven theme (line 3) in this new key. Add your own fingerings.

Double Stop Etude
(Op. 120, No. 7)
Dotzauer
p
mf
9
p
f
Theme from Capriccio Espagnol
Rimsky-Korsakov
Andante con moto
A
B
f
f
ff
ff
LH
LH
12
A
B
A
B
ff
Sarabande
Handel
Andante sostenuto
mf
sim.
f

Theme from Brandenburg Concerto No. 5
J.S. Bach
Allegro
A
B
1
f
f
sim.
9
rit.
rit.
In the Hall of the Mountain King
(from Peer Gynt Suite No. 1)
Grieg
Pìu vivo
A
B
2
ff
ff
1.
2.
div.
spiccato
A
B
mf
mf
f
f
10
A
B
p
cresc. molto
ff
p
cresc. molto
fff
p
cresc. molto
ff
p
cresc. molto
fff

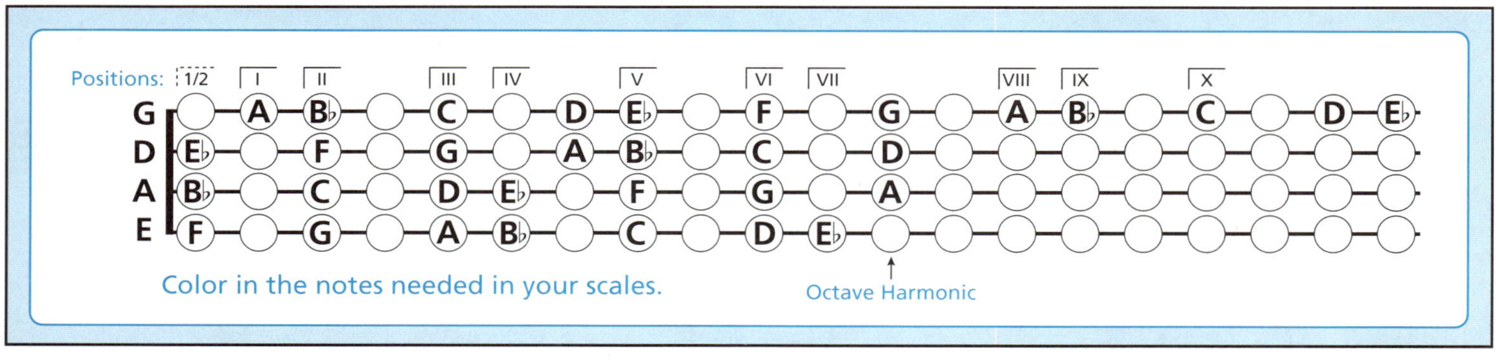

Mark in the half steps (∧)

(a)   (b)   (c)

B♭ Major Scale

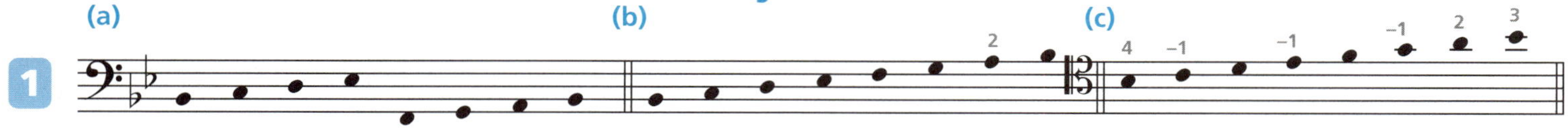

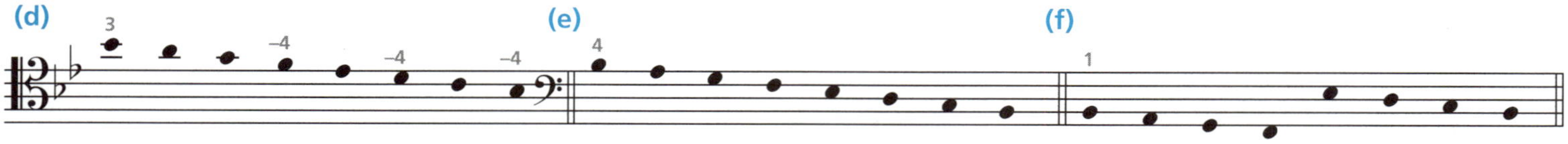

1

(d)   (e)   (f)

Scale in Thirds

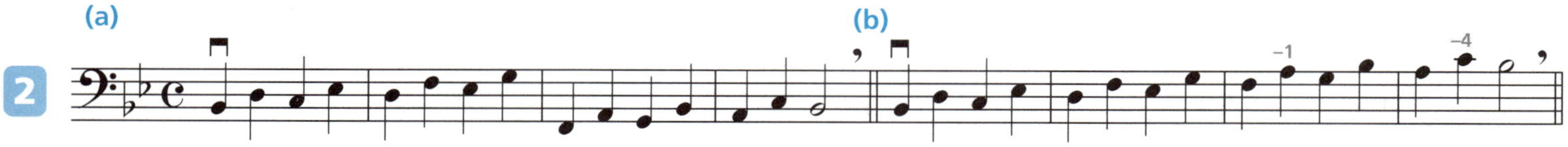

(a)   (b)

2

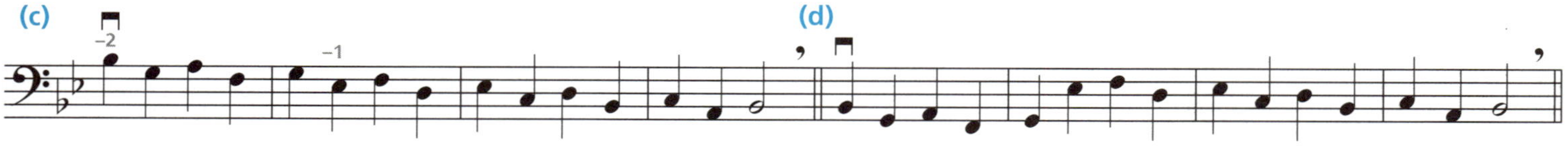

(c)   (d)

I Chord Arpeggio

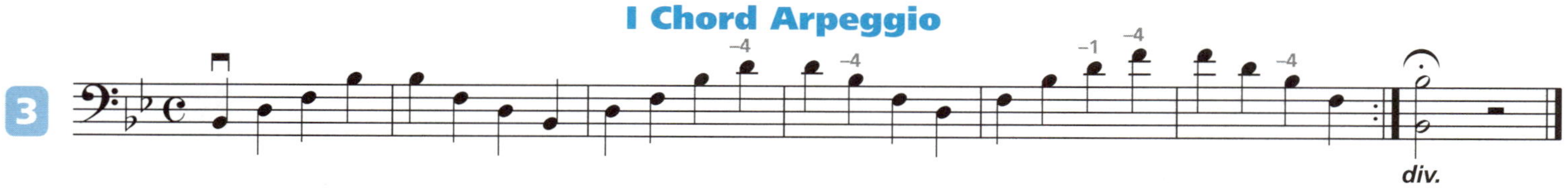

3

div.

IV Chord Arpeggio

V⁷ Chord Arpeggio

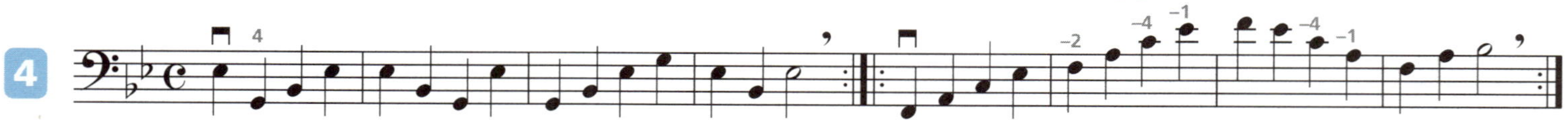

4

Mark in the half steps (∧)

(a)   (b)   (c)   (d)

G Harmonic Minor Scale

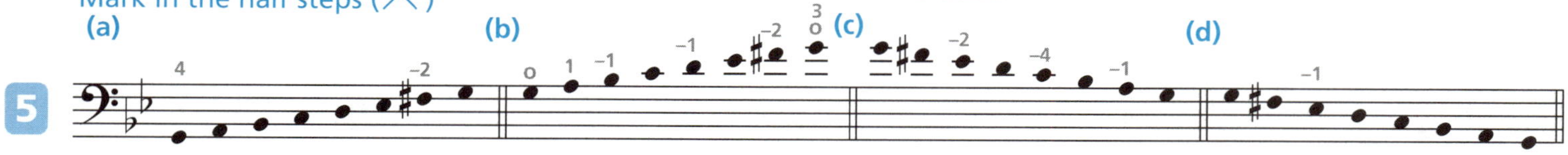

5

i Chord Arpeggio

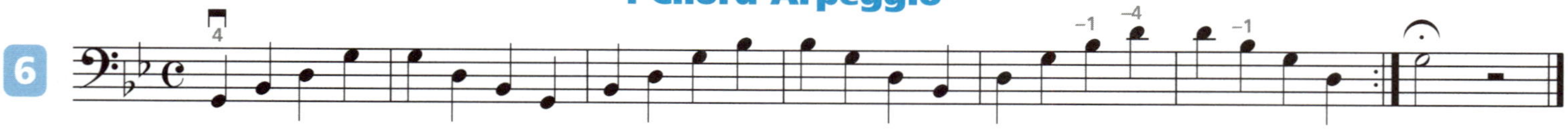

6

iv Chord Arpeggio

V⁷ Chord Arpeggio

7

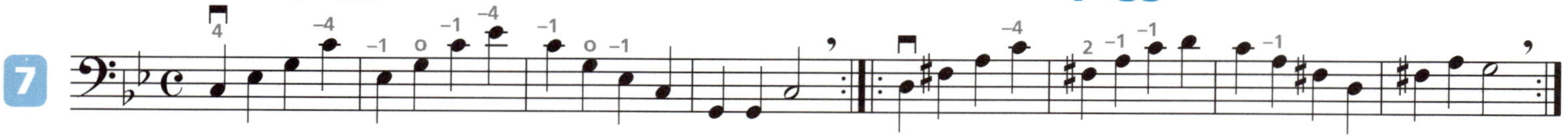

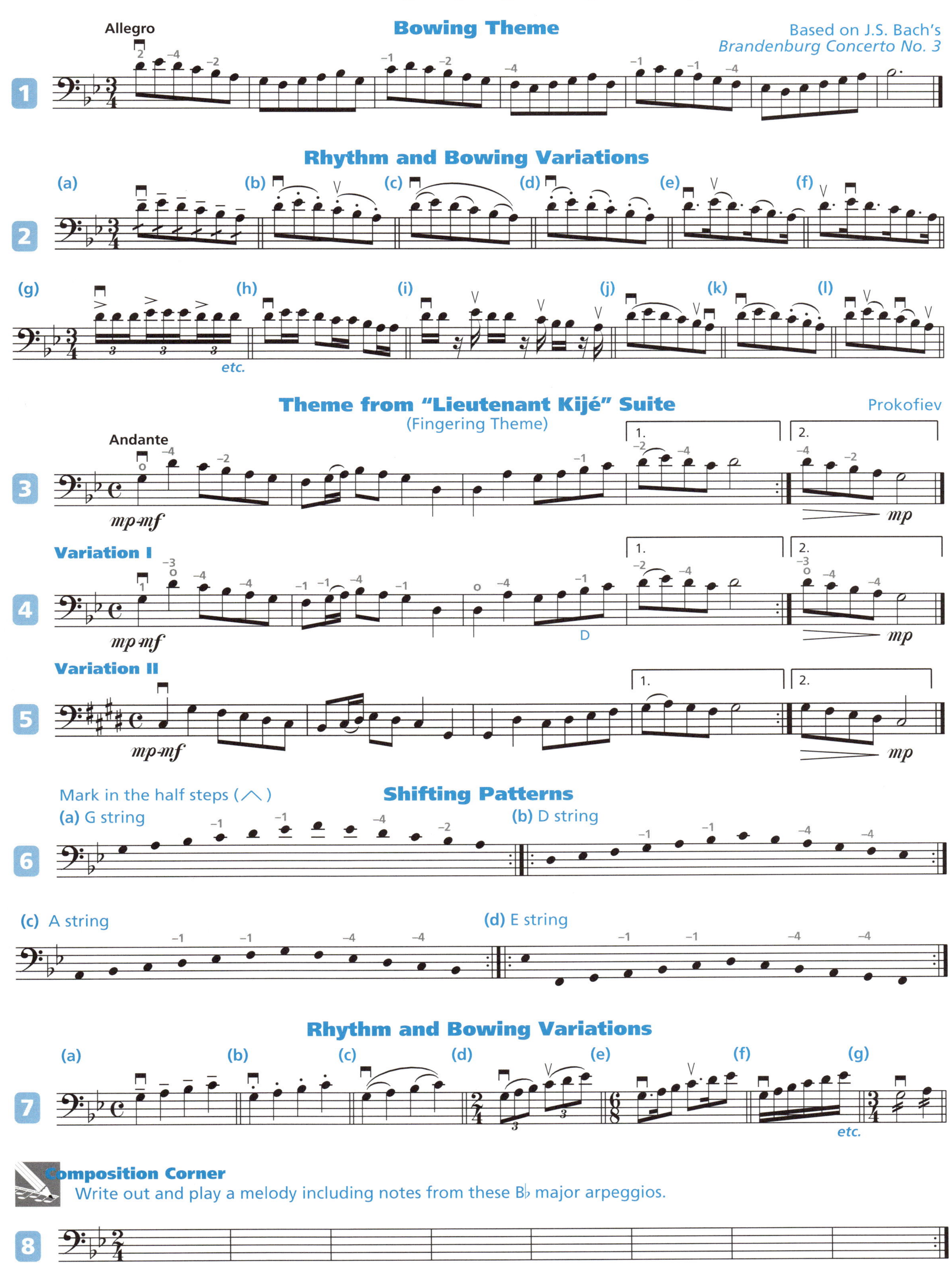
Allegro
Bowing Theme
Based on J.S. Bach's
Brandenburg Concerto No. 3
1

Rhythm and Bowing Variations
(a) (b) (c) (d) (e) (f)
2
(g) (h) (i) (j) (k) (l)
etc.

Theme from "Lieutenant Kijé" Suite
(Fingering Theme)
Prokofiev
Andante
1. 2.
3
mp-mf
mp

Variation I
1. 2.
4
mp-mf
D
mp

Variation II
1. 2.
5
mp-mf
mp

Mark in the half steps (∧)
Shifting Patterns
(a) G string
(b) D string
6

(c) A string
(d) E string

Rhythm and Bowing Variations
(a) (b) (c) (d) (e) (f) (g)
7
etc.

Composition Corner
Write out and play a melody including notes from these B♭ major arpeggios.
8
I   I   IV   I   V7   IV   I   V7

Etude
(Op. 120, No. 2)

Dotzauer

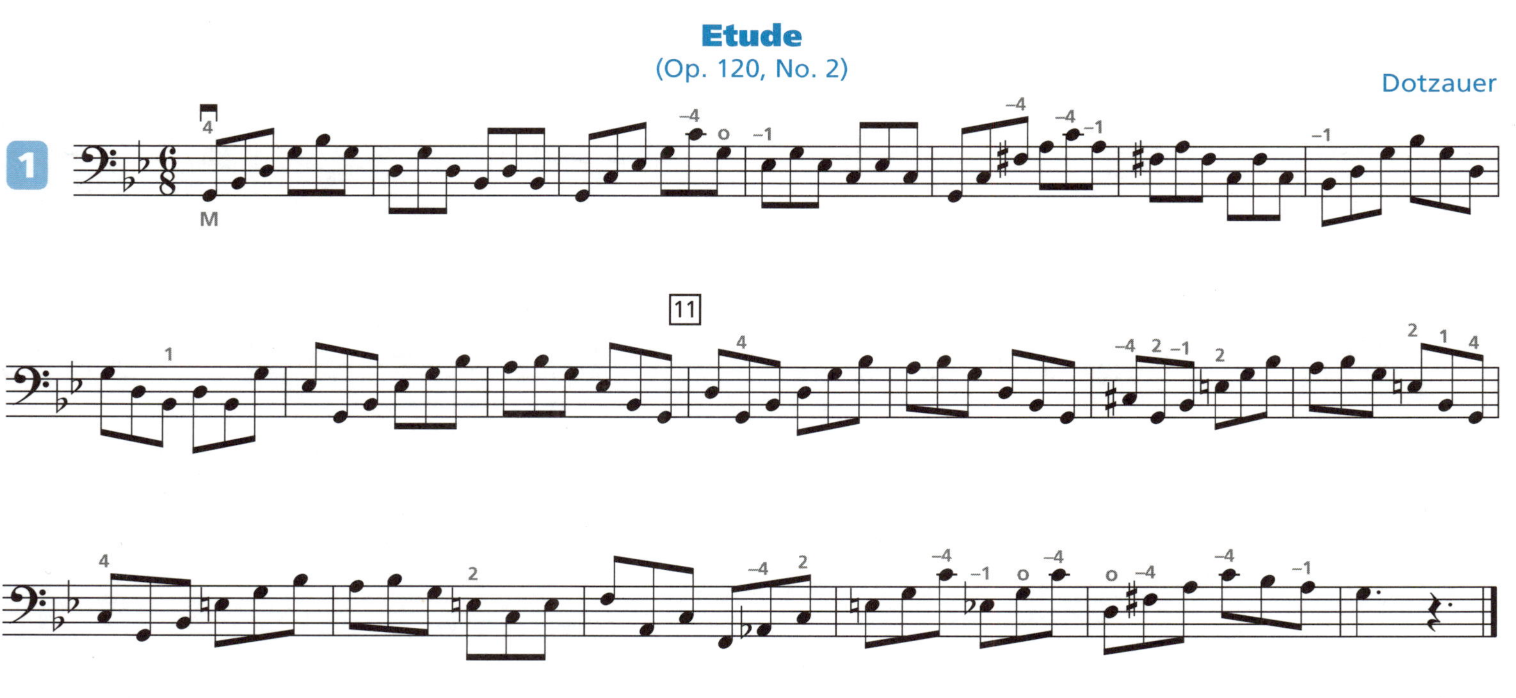

Slavonic Dance No. 8

Dvořák

Fine

Theme from "Pictures at an Exhibition"
(The Great Gate of Kiev)

Mussorgsky

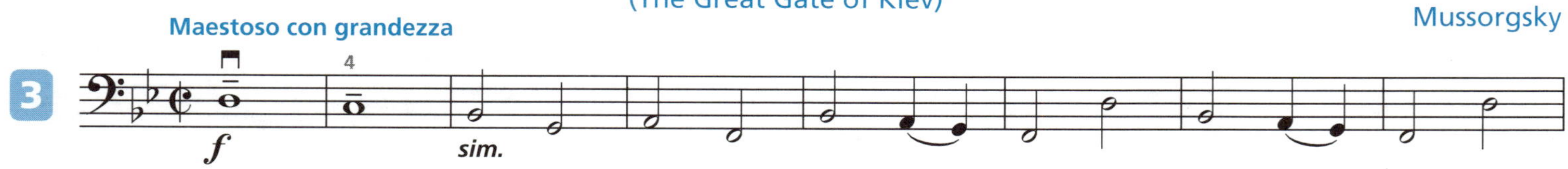

Londonderry Air

Irish Folk Song

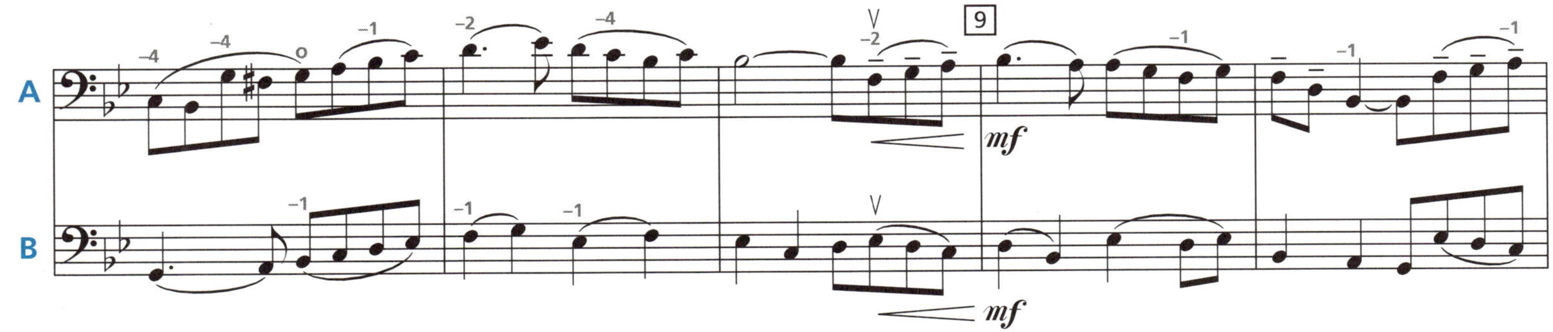

Minuet
(from *Symphony No. 40 in G Minor*, K.550)

Mozart

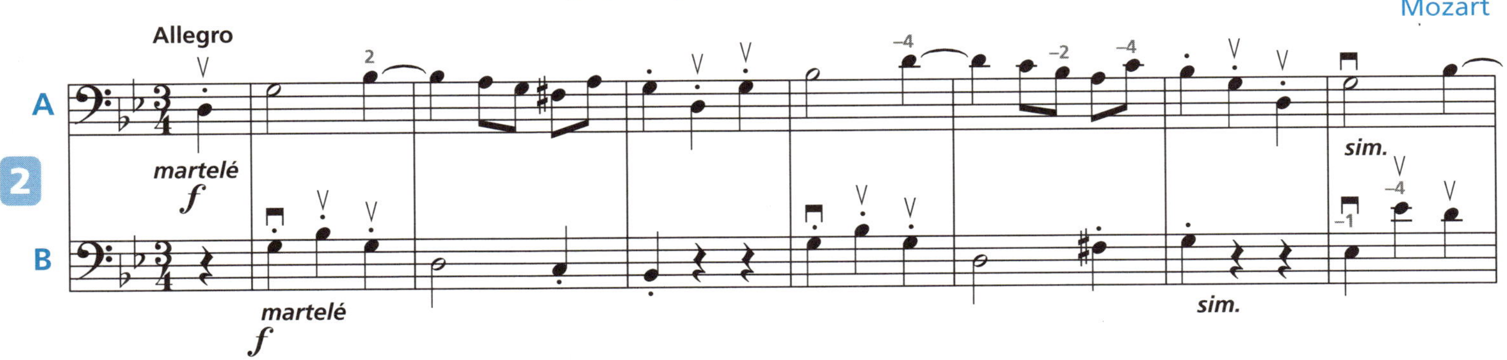

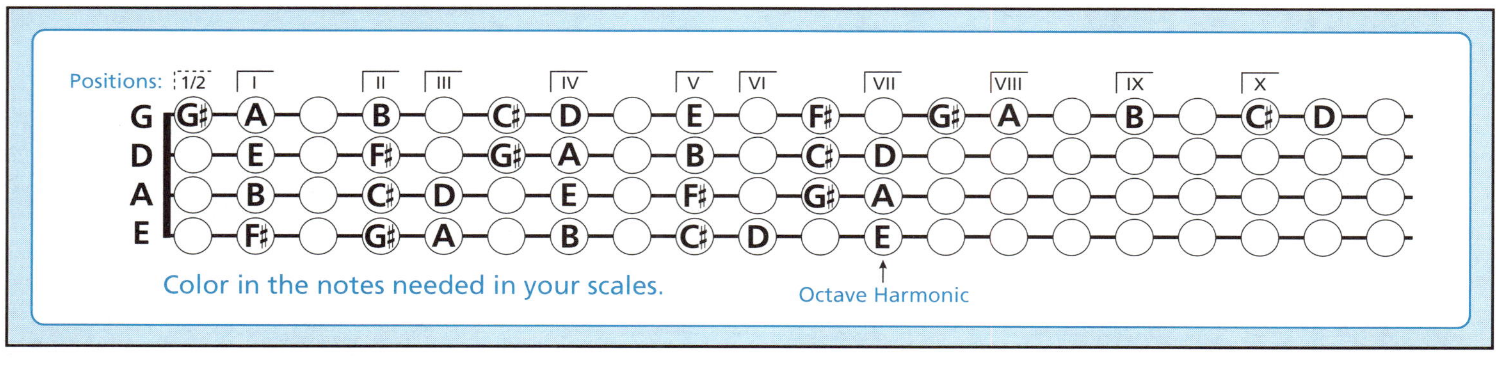

Mark in the half steps (∧)

A Major Scale

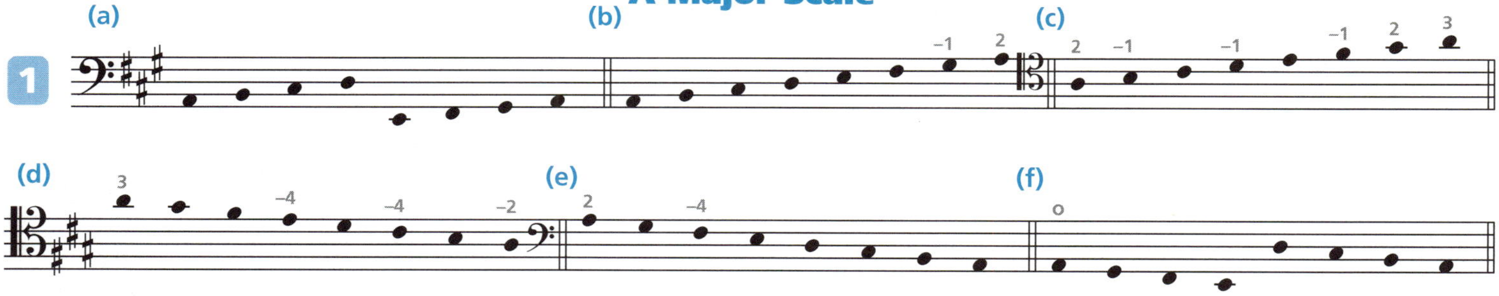

1 (a)   (b)   (c)

(d)   (e)   (f)

Scale in Thirds

2 (a)   (b)

(c)   (d)

I Chord Arpeggio

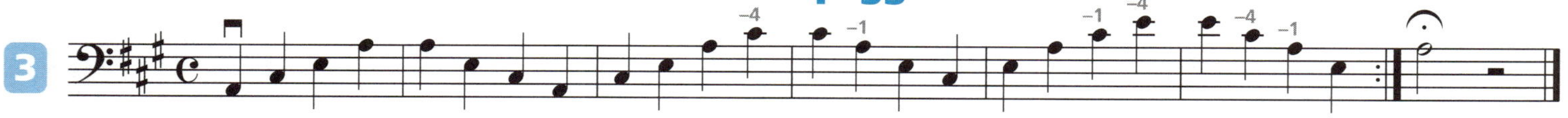

3

IV Chord Arpeggio   V⁷ Chord Arpeggio

4

Mark in the half steps (∧)

F# Melodic Minor Scale

5 (a)   (b)   (c)   (d)

i Chord Arpeggio

6

IV Chord Arpeggio   V⁷ Chord Arpeggio

7

Bowing Theme

Devil's Dream

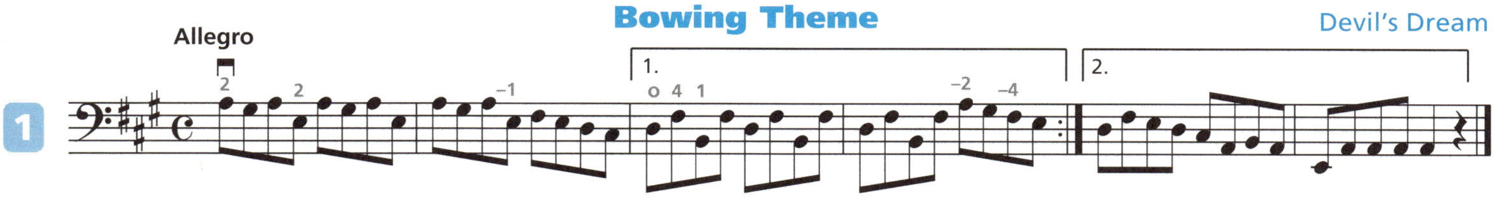

1 Allegro

Rhythm and Bowing Variations

(a) (b) (c) (d) (e) (f)

2 legato · stacc./spicc.

(g) (h) (i) (j) (k) (l)

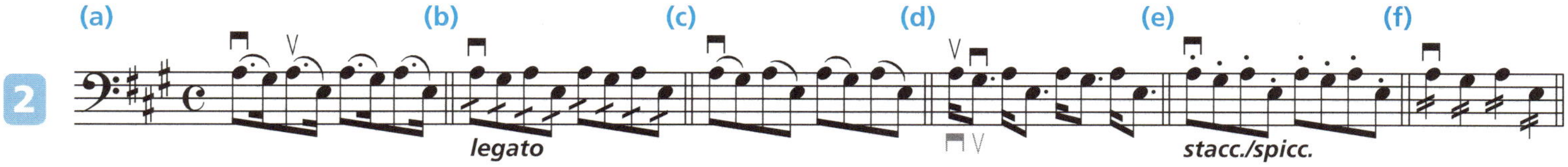

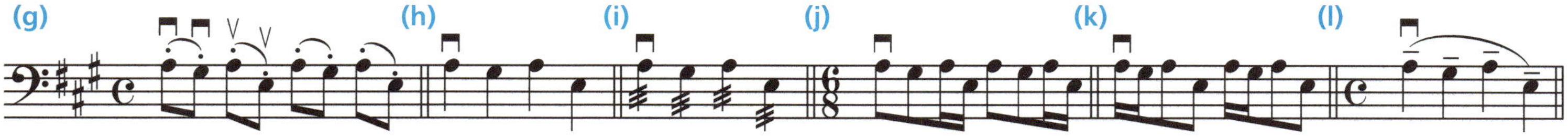

All Through the Night
(Fingering Theme)

Welsh Folk Song

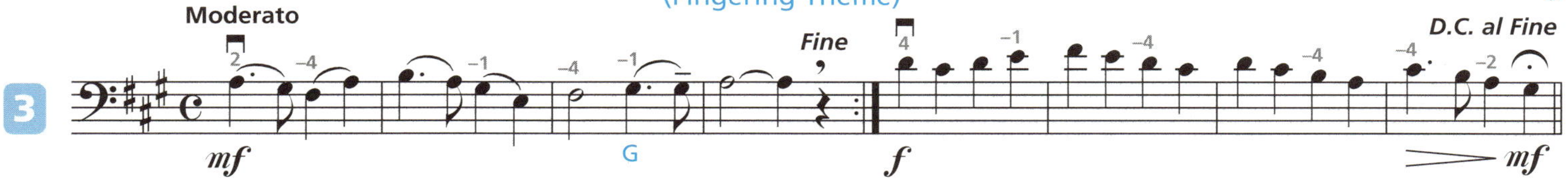

3 Moderato · D.C. al Fine

Variation I

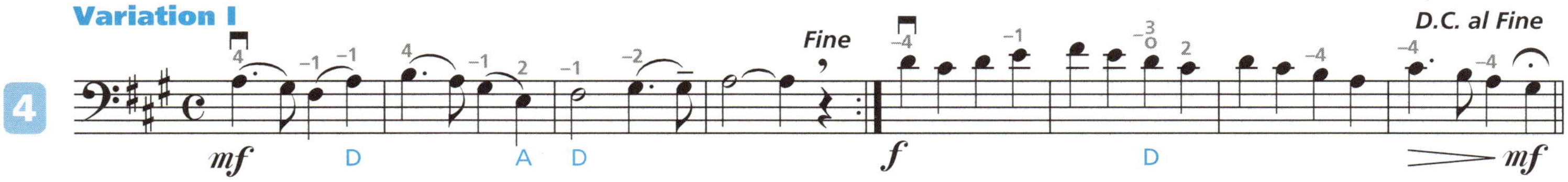

4 D.C. al Fine

Variation II

5 D.C. al Fine

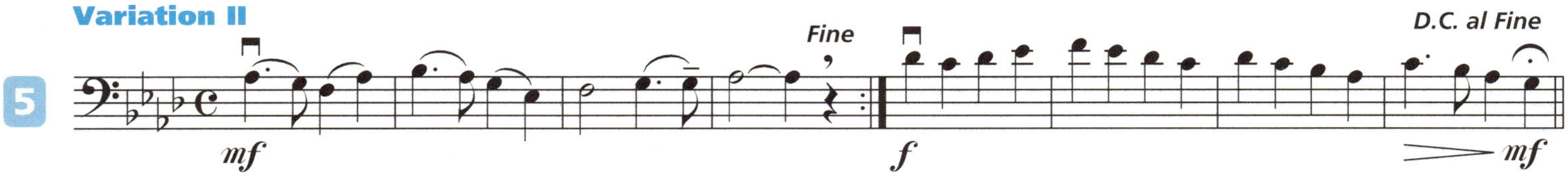

Mark in the half steps (∧) ## Shifting Patterns

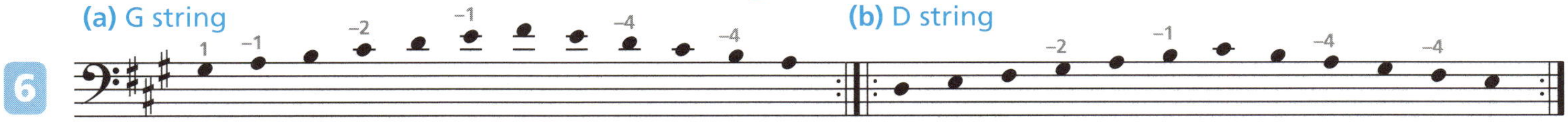

(a) G string (b) D string

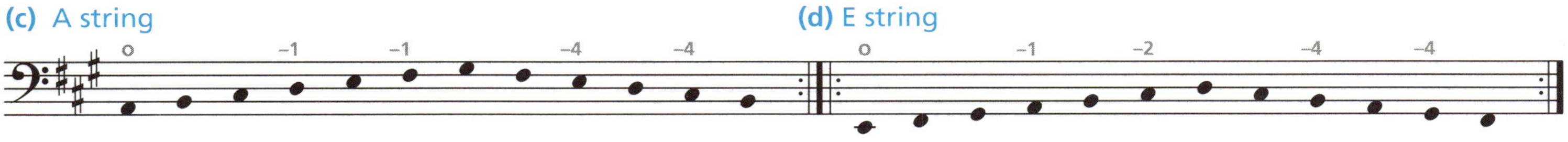

6

(c) A string (d) E string

Rhythm and Bowing Variations

(a) (b) (c) (d) (e) (f) (g)

7 etc.

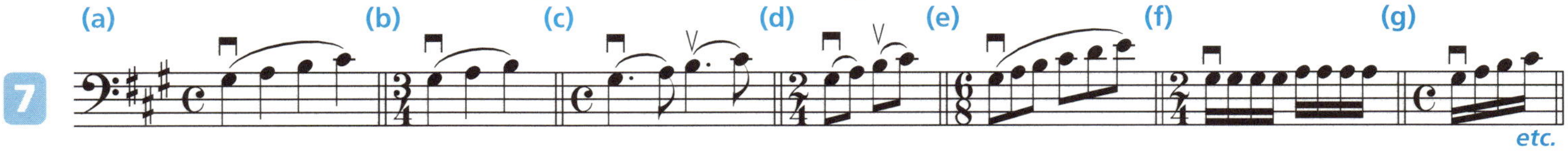

Composition Corner

Write out and play *All Through the Night* in this new key. Add your own fingering and bowing.

Fine D.C. al Fine

8

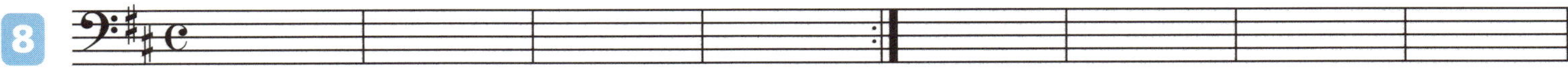

Etude
(Op. 20, No.5)
Kayser
mf

Theme from Symphony No. 29 in A Major
(K. 201)
Mozart
Allegro moderato
p
spiccato ♪'s
sim.
A
B
p
spiccato ♪'s
sim.
tr
mf
D.S. al Coda
p
mf
p
Coda
A
f
B
f

A Mighty Fortress Is Our God
(from Mendelssohn's 5th Symphony)
Largo
Martin Luther
f mp
mf
p
f
rit.
ff

Theme from "A Roman Carnival Overture"

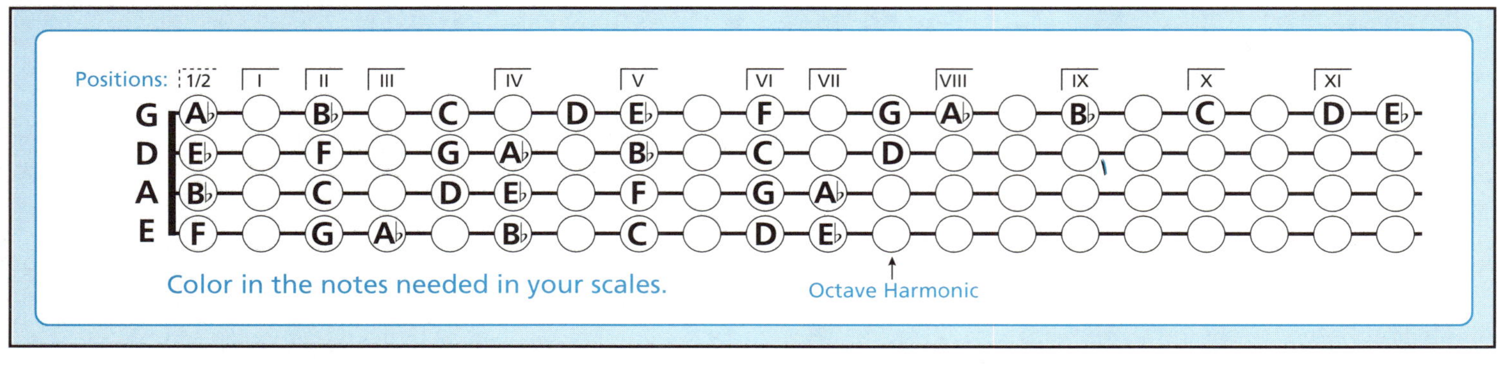

Mark in the half steps (∧)

E♭ Major Scale

(a) (b) (c) (d) (e) (f)

1

Scale in Thirds

(a) (b) (c) (d)

2

I Chord Arpeggio

3

IV Chord Arpeggio

V⁷ Chord Arpeggio

4

Mark in the half steps (∧)

C Harmonic Minor Scale

(a) (b) (c) (d)

5

i Chord Arpeggio

6

iv Chord Arpeggio

V⁷ Chord Arpeggio

7

Bowing Theme
Based on Soldier's Joy
1

Rhythm and Bowing Variations  
(a) (b) (c) (d) (e) (f)
2
(g) (h) (i) (j) (k) (l)
spiccato

Moderato
Blue Bells of Scotland
(Fingering Theme)
Scottish Folk Song
D.S. al Fine
Fine
3
f-p
f

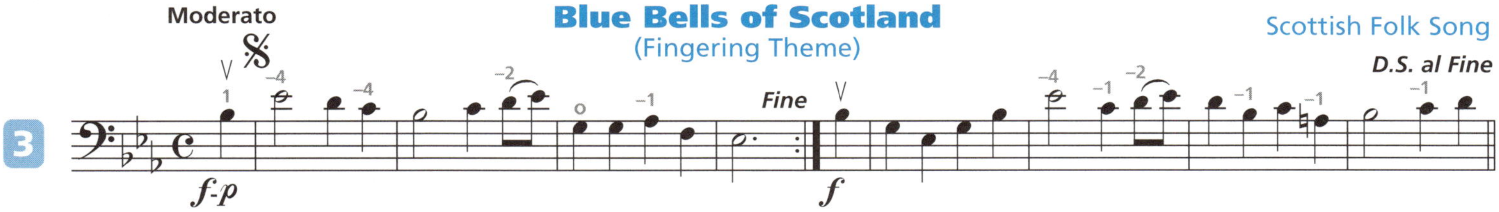

Variation I
Fine
D.S. al Fine
4
D   D G   A   D   D   D   G
f-p
f

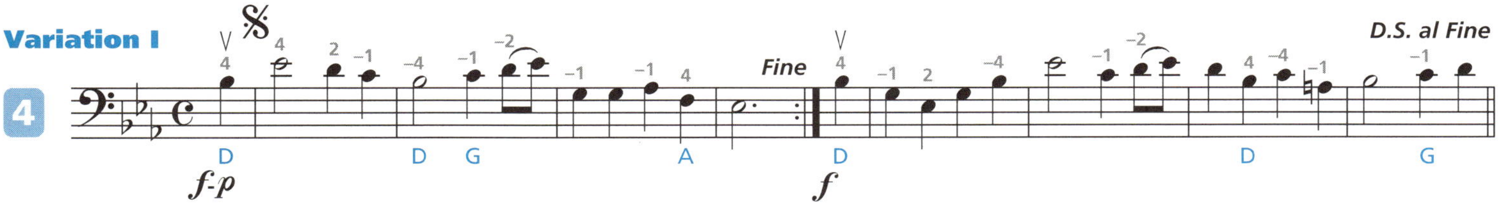

Variation II
Fine
D.S. al Fine
5
f-p
f

Mark in the half steps (⌒)
Shifting Patterns
(a) G string
(b) D string
6

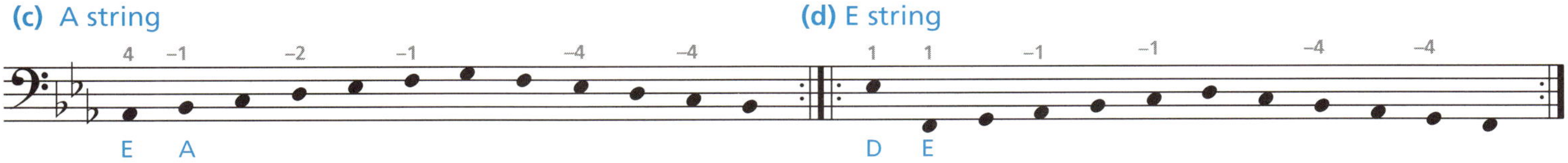

(c) A string
(d) E string
E   A
D   E

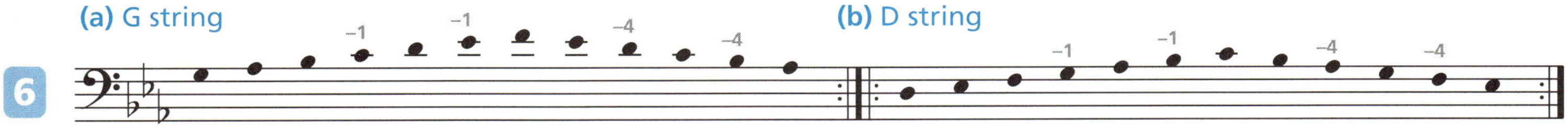

Rhythm and Bowing Variations
(a) (b) (c) (d) (e) (f) (g)
7
etc.

Composition Corner
Write a rhythmic variation for "Blue Bells of Scotland" (line 3).
Fine
D.S. al Fine
8

Etude
(Op. 54, No. 23)

Wolfhart

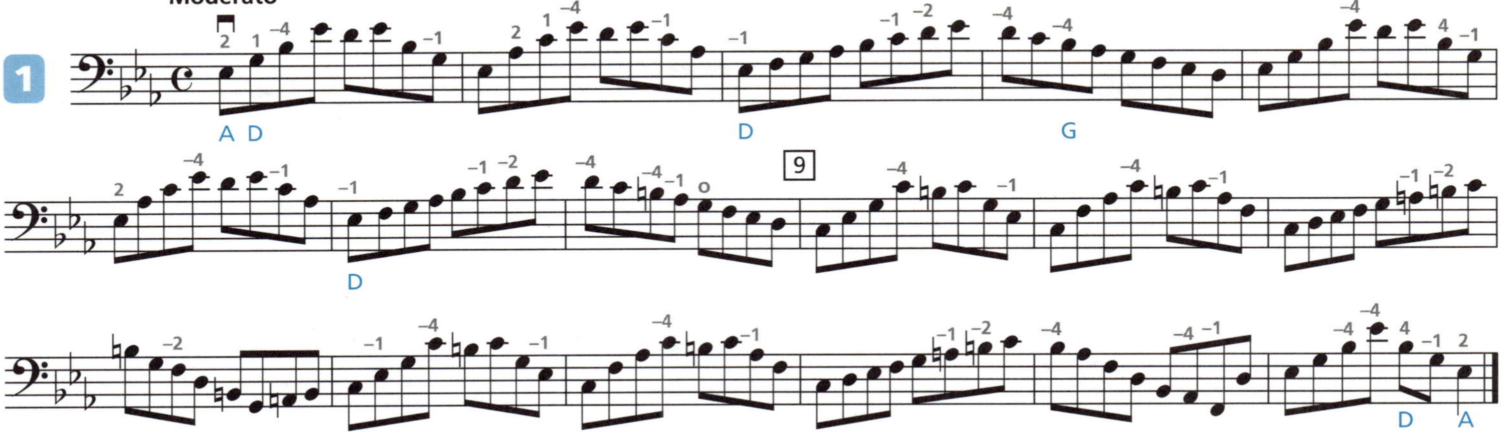

1 Moderato

A D D G
D
D A

Slavonic Dance No. 7 in C Minor

Dvořák

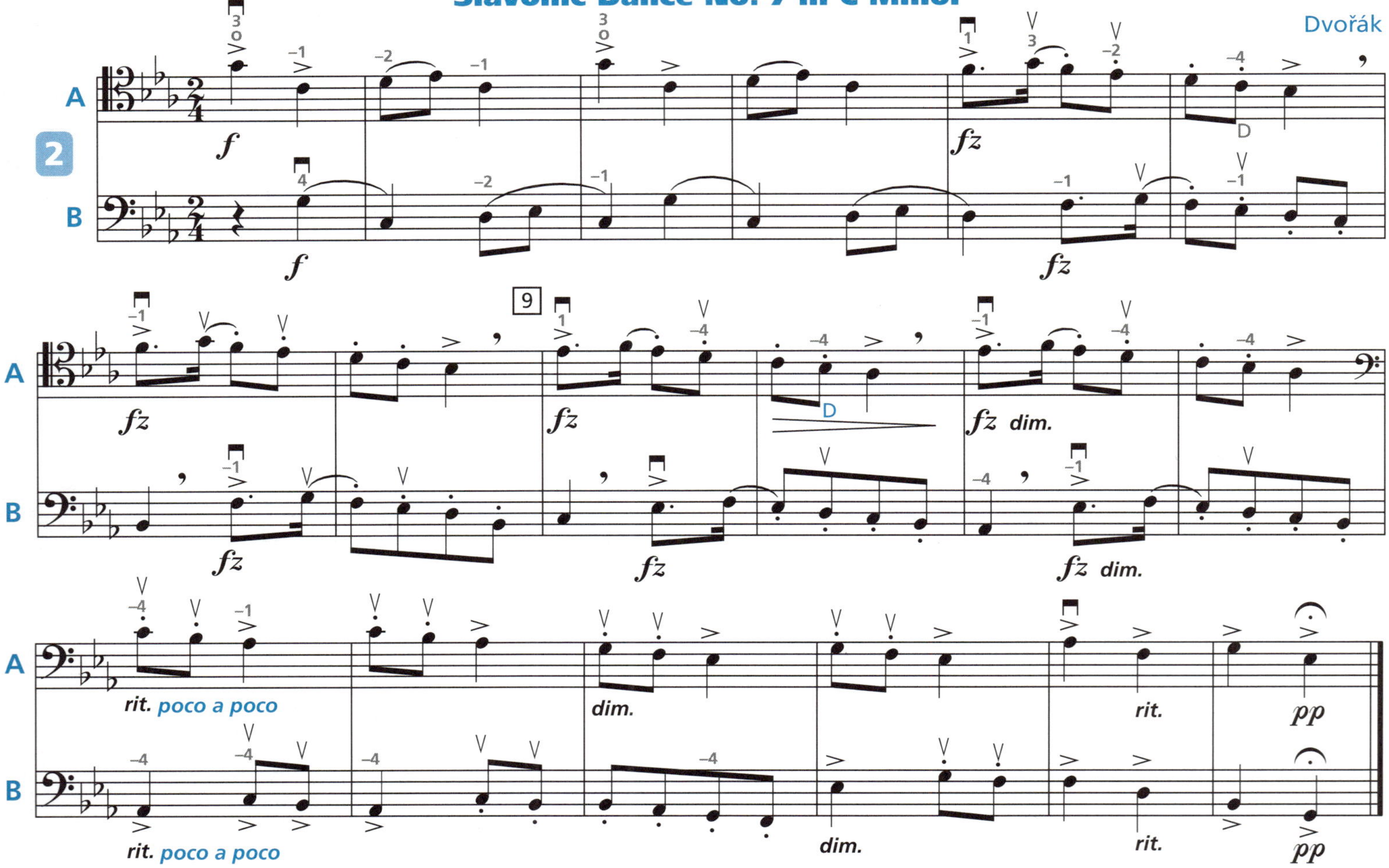

2 Allegro assai

A
B

A
B

A
B

rit. poco a poco dim. rit. *pp*

Chorale from "1812 Overture"
(Op. 49)

Tchaikovsky

3 Largo

cresc. - *ff*

fff LH

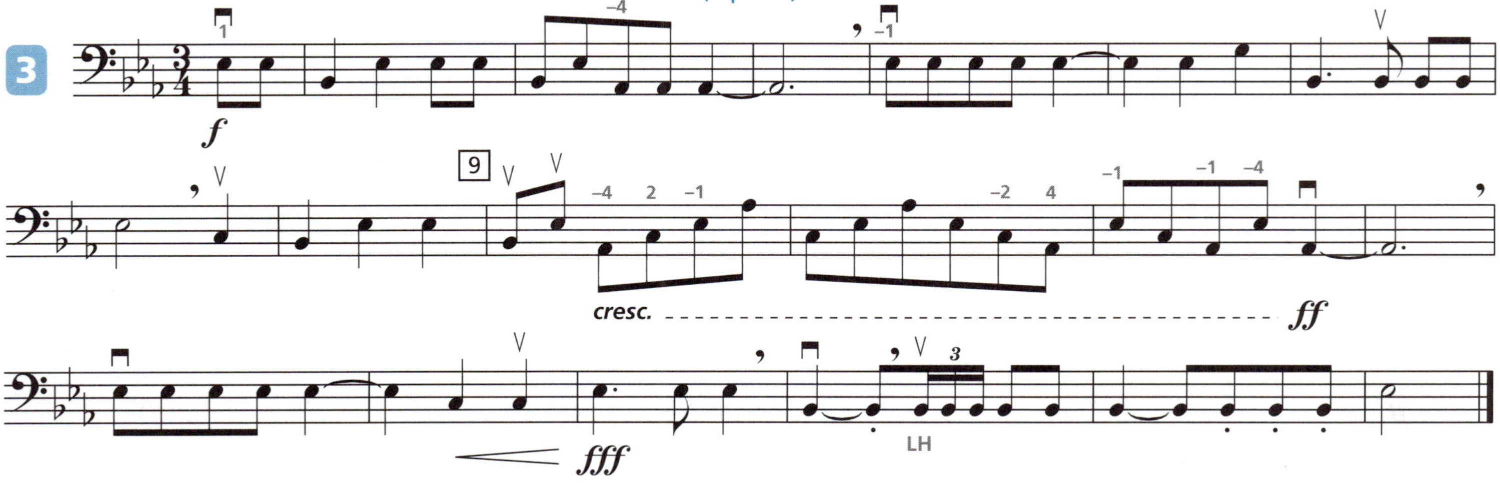

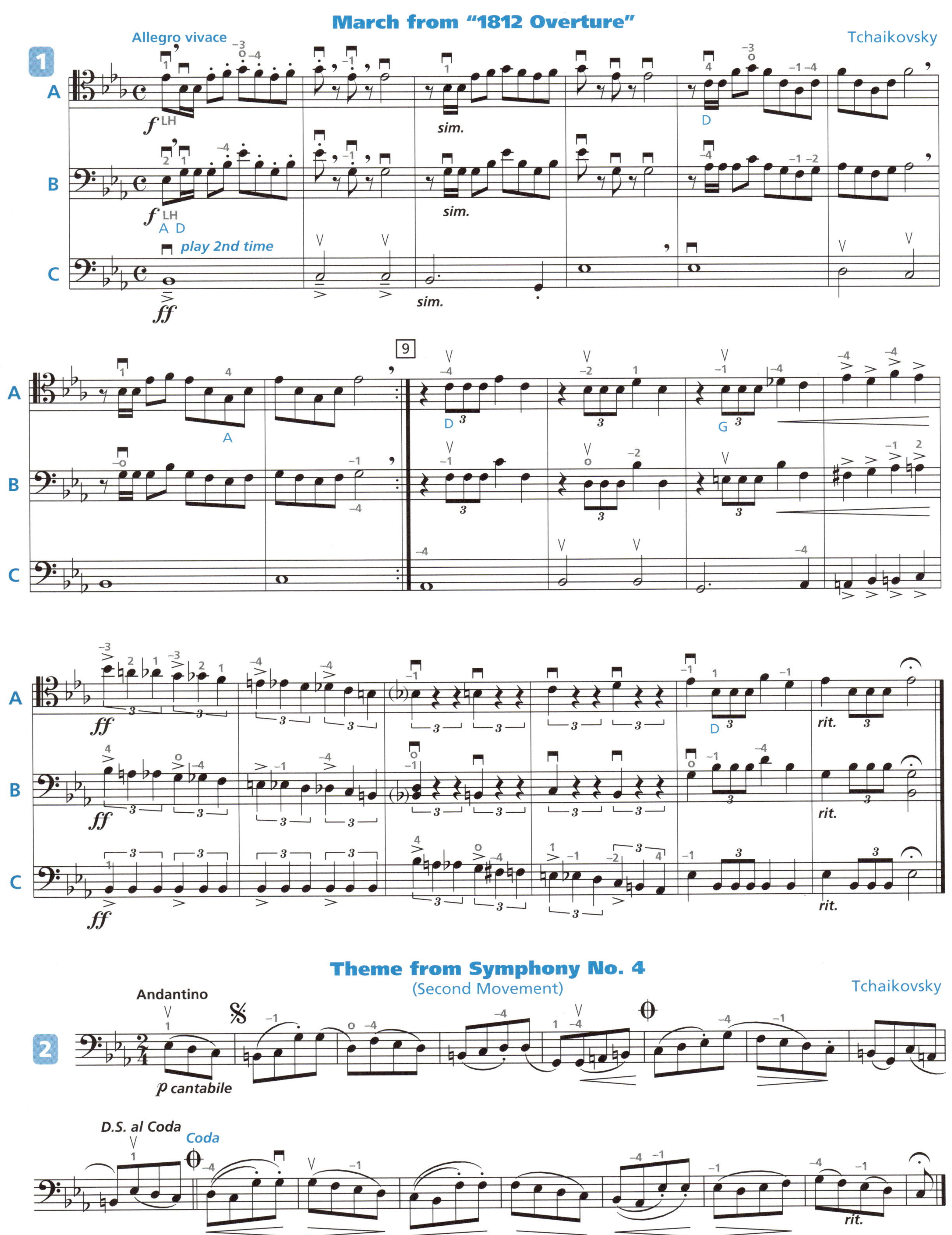
March from "1812 Overture"
Tchaikovsky
Allegro vivace
Theme from Symphony No. 4
(Second Movement)
Tchaikovsky
Andantino
D.S. al Coda
Coda

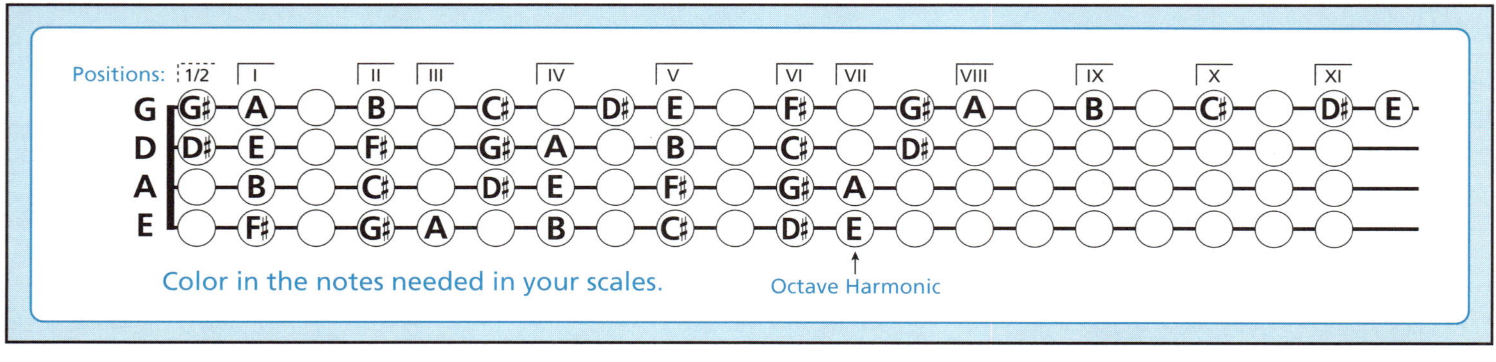

Mark in the half steps (︿)

E Major Scale

(a)   (b)   (c)

1

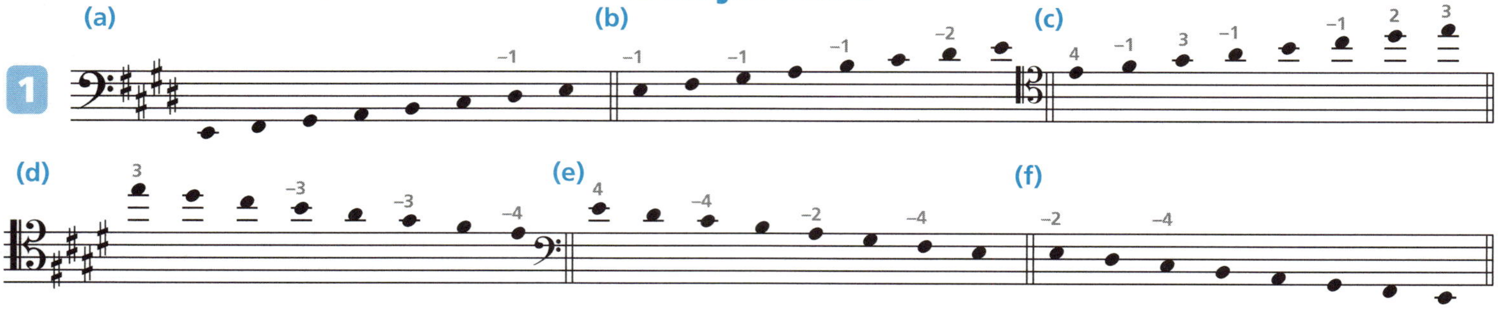

(d)   (e)   (f)

Scale in Thirds

(a)   (b)

2

(c)   (d)

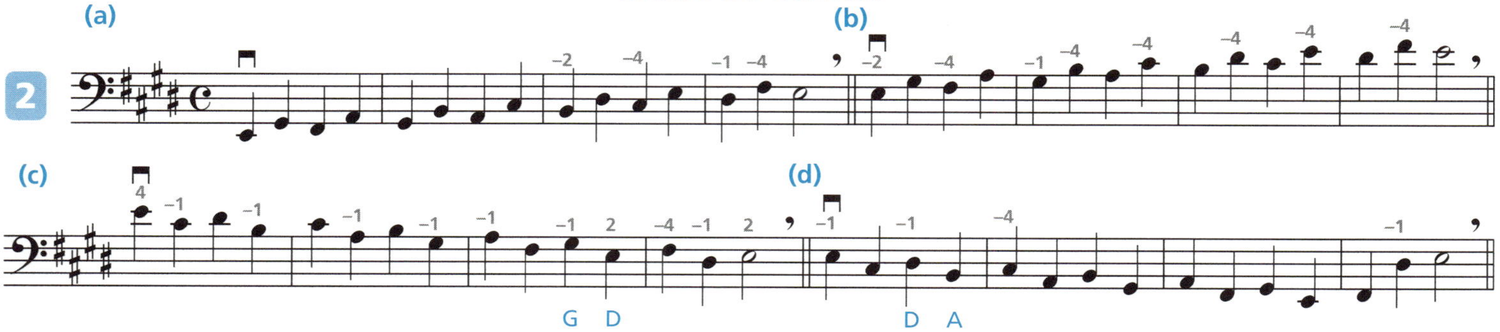

I Chord Arpeggio

3

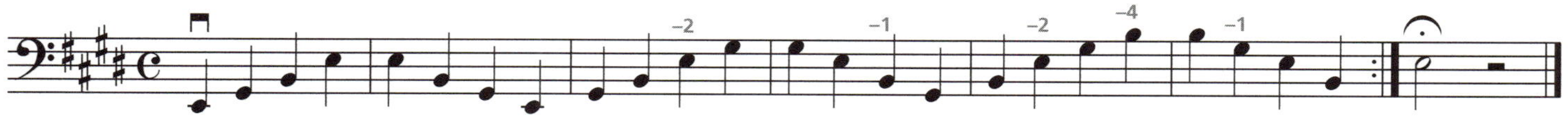

IV Chord Arpeggio   V⁷ Chord Arpeggio

4

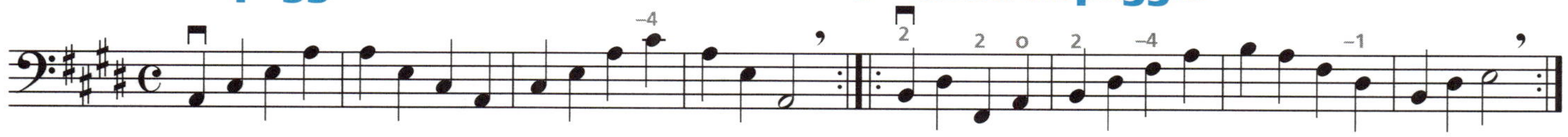

Mark in the half steps (︿)

C# Melodic Minor Scale

(a)   (b)   (c)   (d)

5

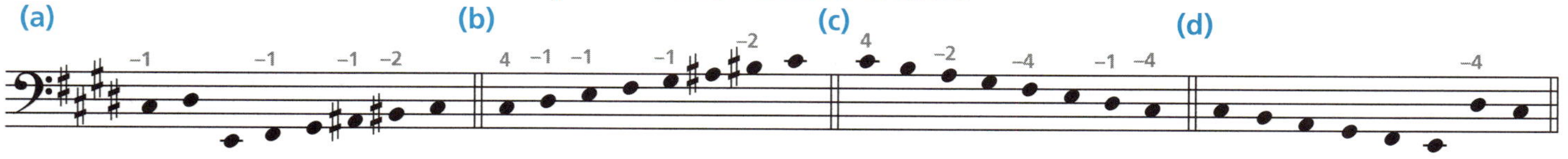

i Chord Arpeggio

6

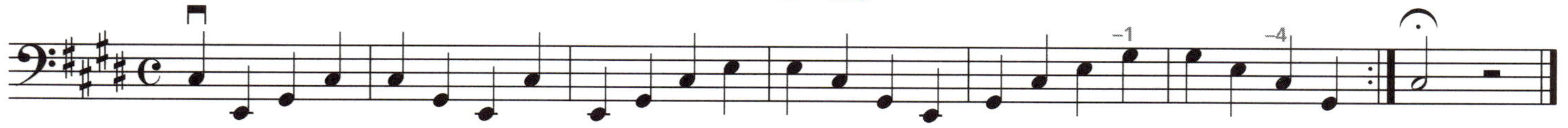

IV Chord Arpeggio   V⁷ Chord Arpeggio

7

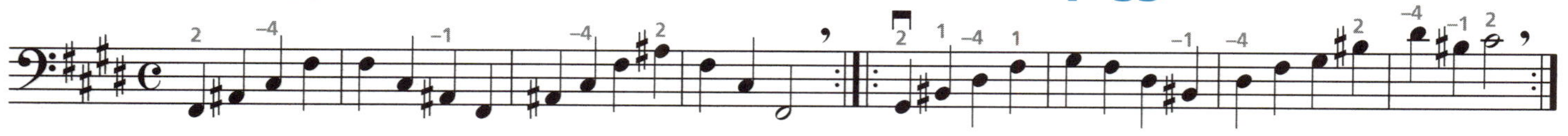

Bowing Theme
Swallow Tail
Irish Jig
G
Rhythm and Bowing Variations
(a) (b) (c) (d) (e) (f)
ricochet
spiccato
(g) (h) (i) (j) (k) (l)
etc.
Ahrirang
(Fingering Theme)
Korean Folk Song
Adagio
mp
Variation I
mp
D
Variation II
mp
Mark in the half steps
Shifting Patterns
(a) G string
(b) D string
(c) A string
(d) E string
Rhythm and Bowing Variations
(a) (b) (c) (d) (e) (f) (g)
Composition Corner
Write and play a duet part for this famous melody.
Fine
D.C. al Fine
I   IV   I   V7   I   V7   I   I   IV   I   V7   I   IV   I   V7

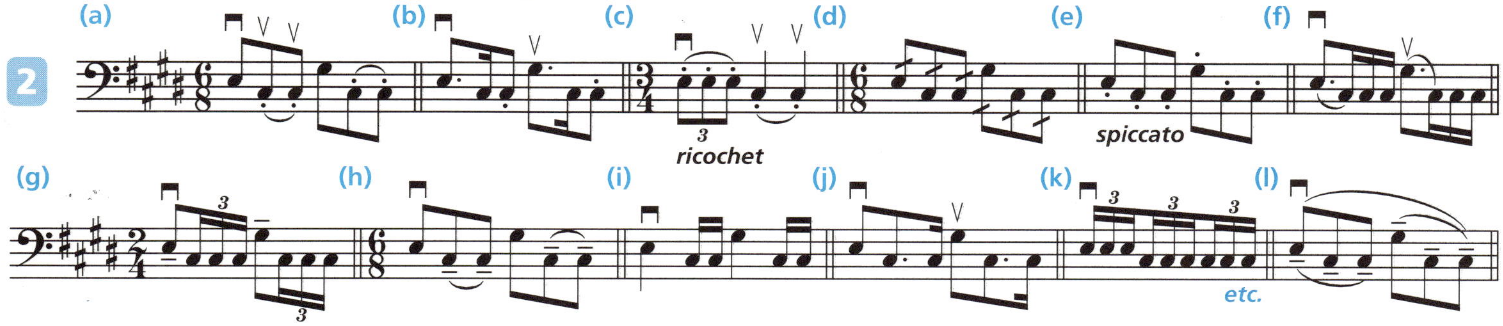

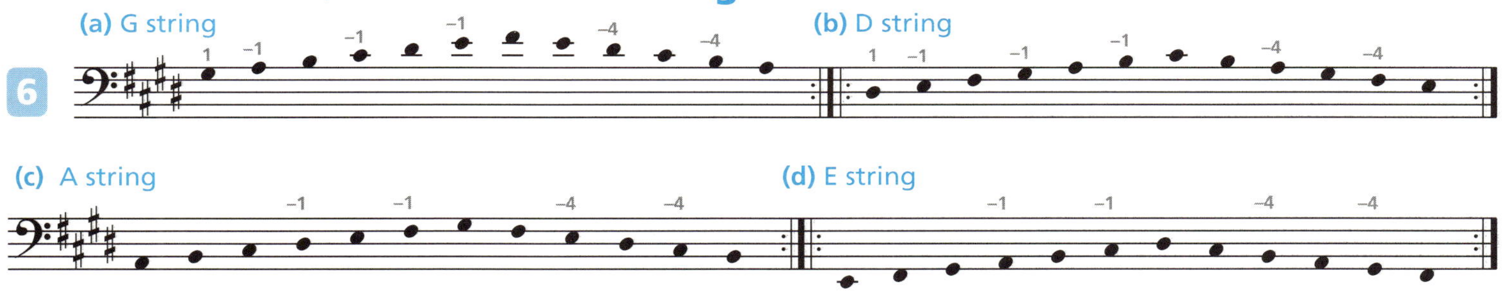

Etude, Duet and Chorale

Rondo
(from Benjamin Britten's
Young Person's Guide to the Orchestra)

Purcell

Allegro maestoso

Theme from "Russian Easter Overture"

Rimsky-Korsakov

Sostenuto

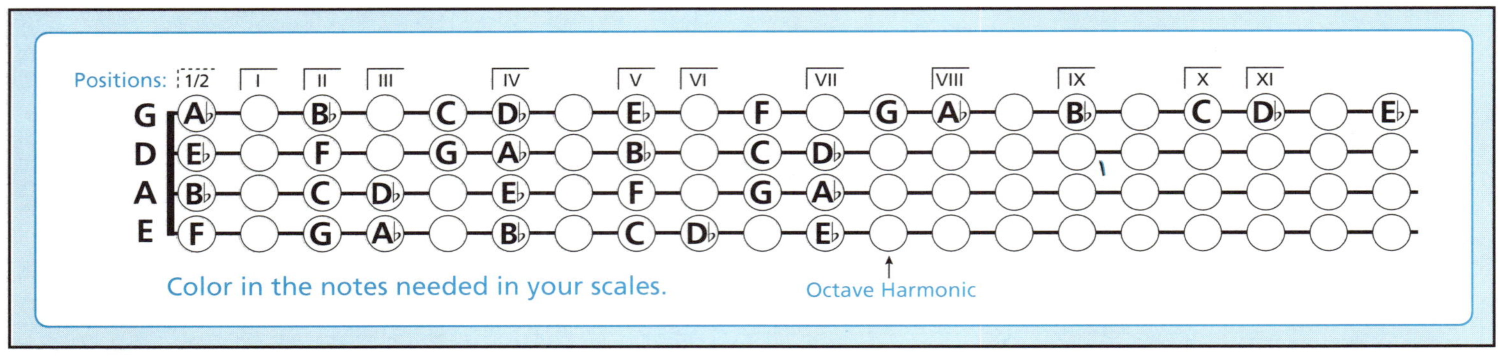

Mark in the half steps (⌒)

A♭ Major Scale

(a) (b) (c)

1

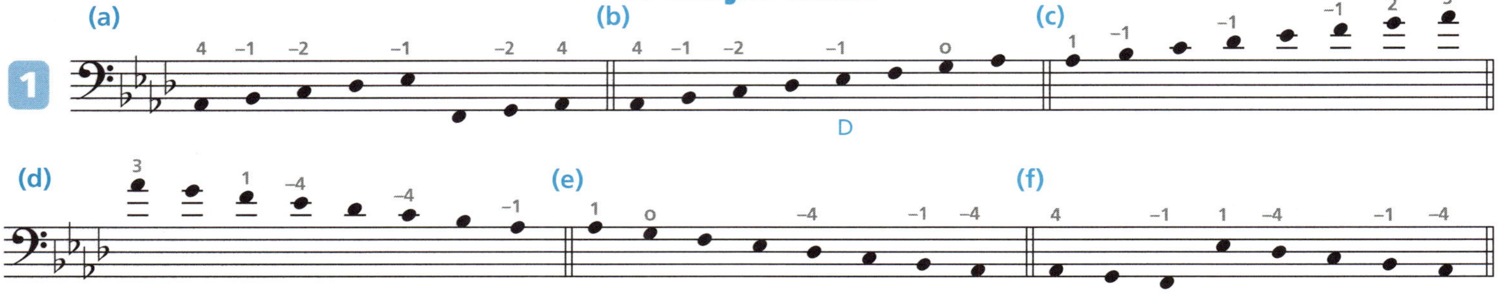

(d) (e) (f)

Scale in Thirds

(a) (b)

2

(c) (d)

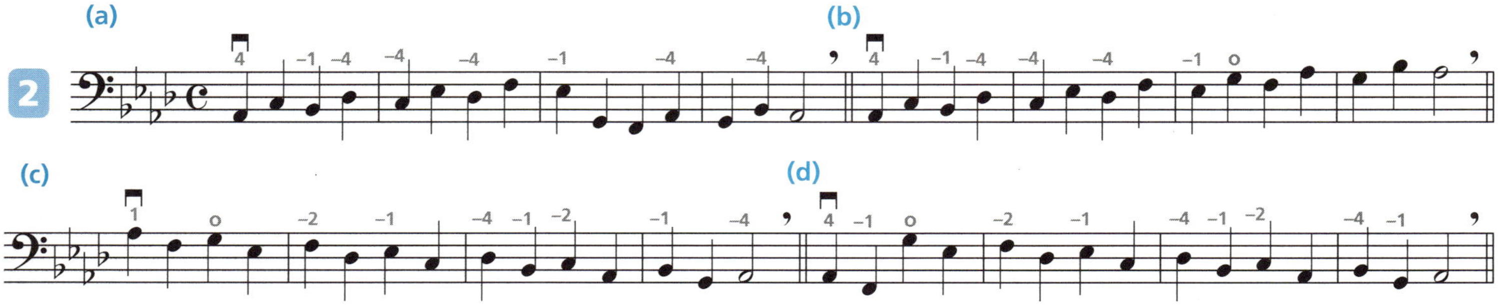

I Chord Arpeggio

3

IV Chord Arpeggio

V⁷ Chord Arpeggio

4

Mark in the half steps (⌒)

F Harmonic Minor Scale

(a) (b) (c) (d)

5

i Chord Arpeggio

6

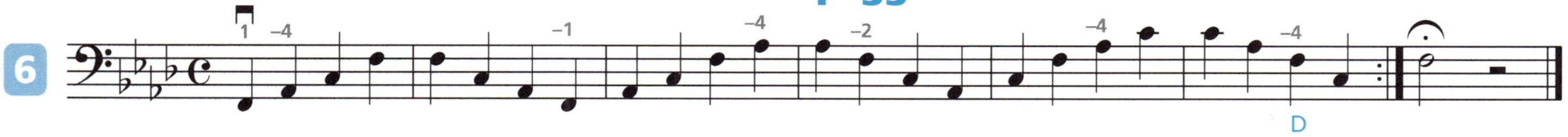

iv Chord Arpeggio

V⁷ Chord Arpeggio

7

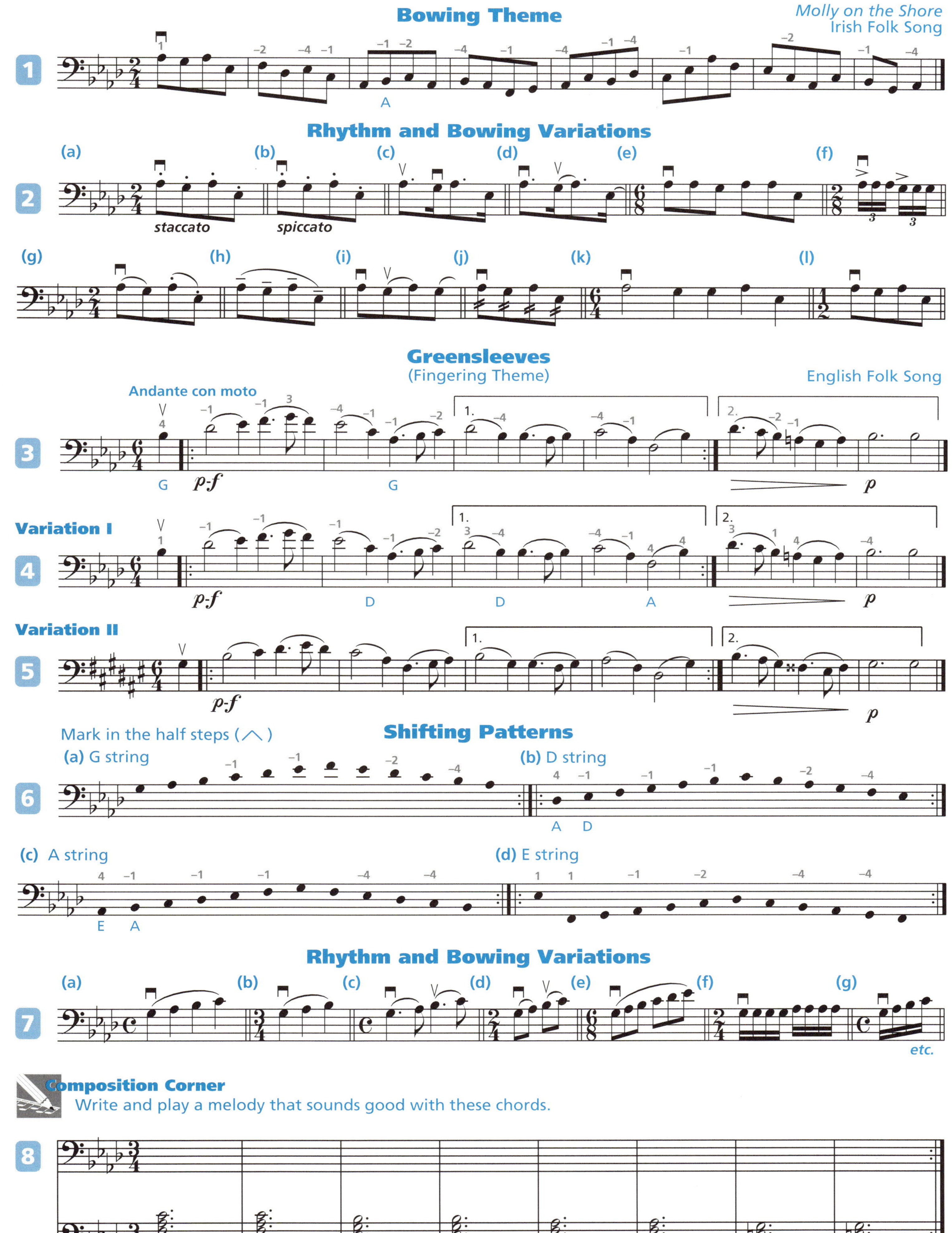
Bowing Theme
Molly on the Shore
Irish Folk Song
1
A
Rhythm and Bowing Variations
(a) (b) (c) (d) (e) (f)
staccato   spiccato
2
3   3
(g) (h) (i) (j) (k) (l)
Greensleeves
(Fingering Theme)
English Folk Song
Andante con moto
3
G   p-f   G   p
Variation I
4
p-f   D   D   A   p
Variation II
5
p-f   p
Mark in the half steps (⌃)   Shifting Patterns
(a) G string   (b) D string
6
A   D
(c) A string   (d) E string
E   A
Rhythm and Bowing Variations
(a) (b) (c) (d) (e) (f) (g)
7
etc.
Composition Corner
Write and play a melody that sounds good with these chords.
8

Etude in A♭ Major

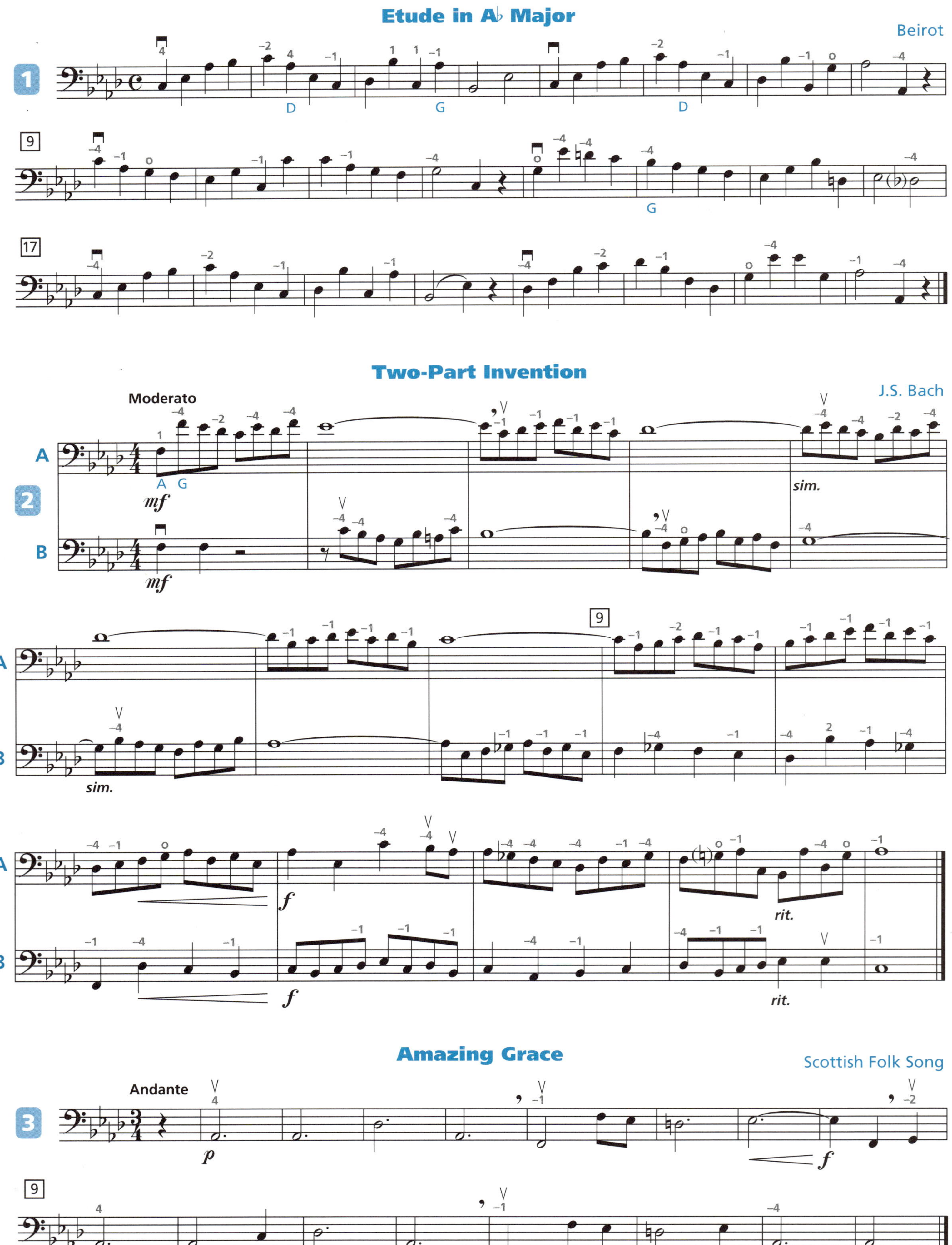

Andante sostenuto
Finlandia
Sibelius
mf espressivo
p
10
G
D
G
18
ff
f
D
f
p
rit.
rit.
Andante cantabile
Dives and Lazarus
English Folk Song
mp
p
9
mf
A
mp
mp
rit.
p
rit.

Clef Reference

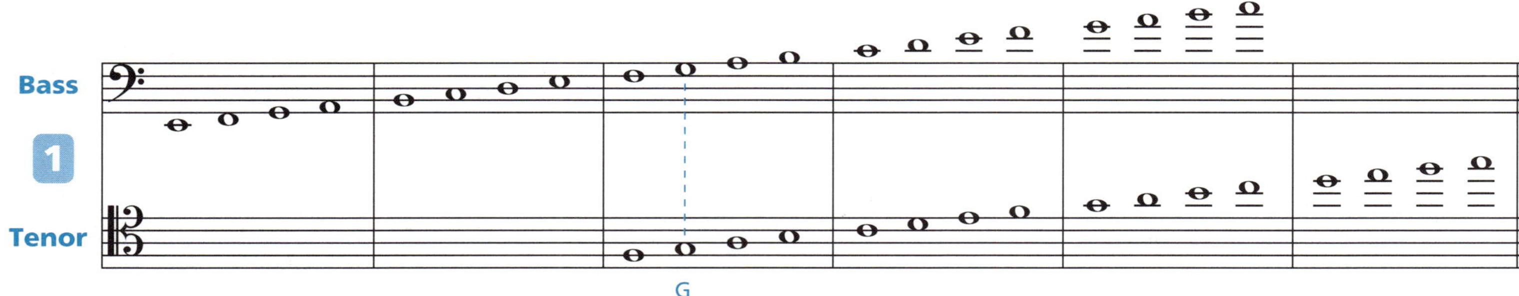

Clef Practice

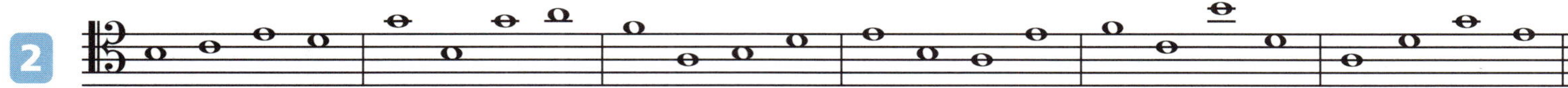

Crazy Clefs

Thumb Position Studies

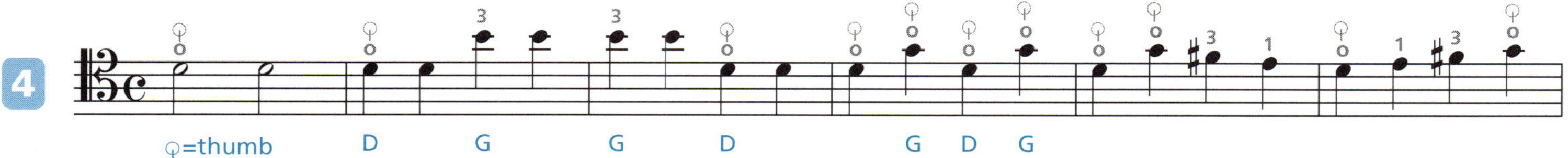

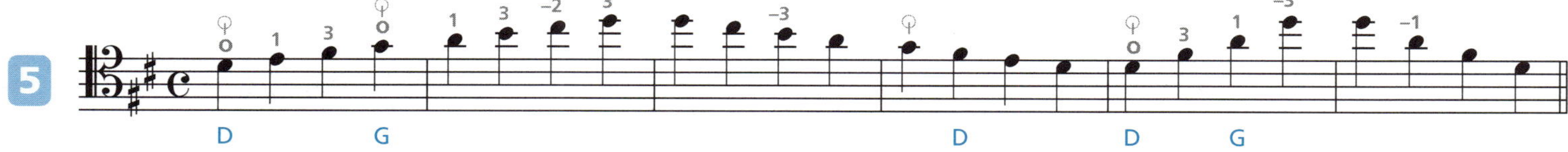

French Folk Song

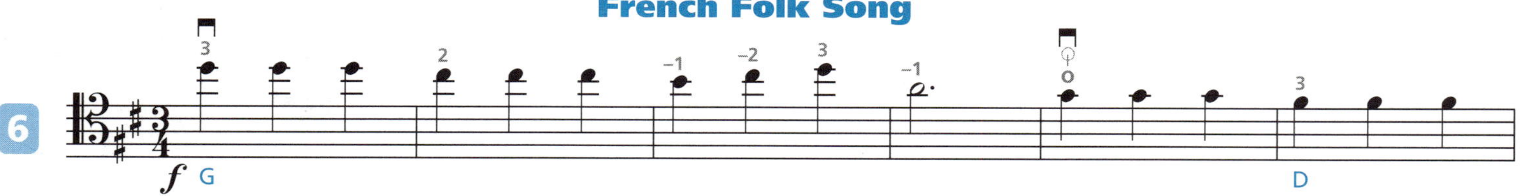

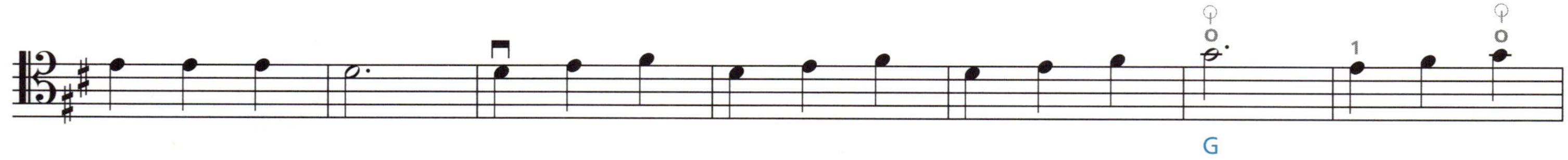

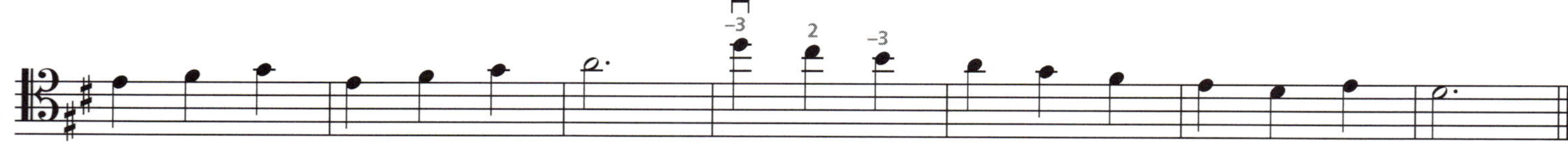

"Klangfarben Kanon"
Adapted from G.P. Telemann
Allegro
*
f
1.
2.
14
Fine
p
22
D.C. al Fine
Open String Rhapsody
Moderato
ff
mf
9
p
f
Fine
17
pp
mp
pp
25
D.C. al Fine
cresc.
rit.

GLOSSARY

ADAGIO Slow and leisurely. Slow movement of a long work of music.

ALLEGRETTO GRAZIOSO Lively and gracefully.

ALLEGRETTO NON TROPPO Moderately fast but not too fast.

ALLEGRO ASSAI Very fast.

ALLEGRO FEROCE Fast and furious.

ALLEGRO GIOCOSO Fast and joyous.

ALLEGRO MAESTOSO Fast and majestic.

ALLEGRO MODERATO Moderately fast.

ALLEGRO MA NON TROPPO Fast but not too fast.

ALLEGRO VIVACE Fast and lively.

ANDANTE CANTABILE Slowly, in a singing style.

ANDANTE CON MOTO Slow with motion.

ANDANTE DOLOROSO Slowly expressing pain or grief.

ANDANTE SOSTENUTO Slowly in smooth, legato style.

ARPEGGIOS A chord with notes played one at a time.

ASSAI Very.

CANON Imitation form where two or more parts are played successively.

CHORD A series of tones played simultaneously.

> **I CHORD** (Tonic) Chord built on the first degree of the scale using intervals of a 3rd and a 5th.
>
> **IV CHORD** (Sub-dominant) Chord built on the fourth degree of a scale using intervals of a 3rd and a 5th.
>
> **V7 CHORD** (Dominant 7th) Chord built on the fifth degree of the scale using intervals of a 3rd, 5th and 7th.

CODA The ending of a piece, passage or movement.

CONCERTO A piece in several movements written for a solo instrument accompanied by orchestra.

CRESCENDO MOLTO Get much louder.

DOUBLE STOP Playing on two strings at a time.

ETUDE A composition written to help improve technique.

ESPRESSIVO Play expressively.

FUGUE A musical form based on interwoven melodies.

HARMONIC MINOR SCALE A natural minor scale with a raised 7th degree.

JIG A lively dance form often found in music from England, Scotland and Ireland.

MAESTOSO CON GRANDEZZA Majestic with grandeur.

MELODIC MINOR SCALE A natural minor scale with a raised 6th and 7th ascending and natural minor descending.

MOLTO Very much.

MOVEMENT A particular principal section of a longer composition such as a symphony, concerto or sonata.

OVERTURE An introduction to an opera, play or ballet.

PIÙ More.

PIÙ VIVO More spirited.

POCO A POCO Little by little.

PRESTO Faster than allegro.

SYMPHONY A long piece written for an orchestra composed of three to five movements.

THUMB POSITION Playing notes with the thumb (cello and bass).

TRILL (*tr* or *tr*⌇⌇⌇) Rapid alternation of two notes.

TWO-PART INVENTION An imitation form often used by J. S. Bach where both parts are treated equally.

HISTORY AND COMPOSER TIMELINE

Renaissance Period (1450–1600)

Renaissance means "rebirth," symbolizing a revival of all the arts during this era. Music of this time, including masses, motets and chorales, was mostly used for religious purposes such as the chorales of Martin Luther.

Martin Luther (1483–1546)—p. 24

Baroque Period (1600–1750)

Baroque music contains driving rhythms and staccato bowing styles. During this time, instrumental music flourished. Two of the most famous composers of this period are J. S. Bach and G. F. Handel. Along with many other composers they composed prolifically for strings.

Henry Purcell (1659–1695)—p. 33
Antonio Vivaldi (1678–1741)—p. 32
George Phillip Telemann (1681–1767)—p. 39
Johann Sebastian Bach (1685–1750)—p. 12, 17, 19, 32, 36
George Frederick Handel (1685–1759)—p. 16

Classical Period (1750–1830)

Haydn is credited with the development of Classical style. He is considered to be the father of the symphony and the string quartet. Mozart, Beethoven and Schubert also composed in these forms and in a style which utilized spiccato bowing.

Wolfgang Amadeus Mozart (1756–1791)—p. 21, 24
Ludwig van Beethoven (1770–1827)—p. 13, 15
Franz Schubert (1799–1838)—p. 8

Romantic Period (1830–1900)

Music in the Romantic period was known for expressive melodies and dramatic climaxes. Harmonies and rhythms became more complex and the modern symphony orchestra was established. Much of this music is nationalistic and is based on folk music traditions.

Hector Berlioz (1803–1869)—p. 5, 25
Georges Bizet (1838–1875)—p. 4, 25
Modest Mussorgsky (1839–1881)—p. 13, 20
Peter I. Tchaikovsky (1840–1893)—p. 28, 29
Antonin Dvořák (1841–1904)—p. 4, 9, 20, 28
Edward Grieg (1843–1907)—p. 12, 17
Niccolai Rimsky-Korsakov (1844–1908)—p. 16, 33
Jean Sibelius (1865–1907)—p. 37

Contemporary Period (1900–2000)

The Contemporary period (20th Century) is an era of great innovation and experimentation. Along with the development of older forms, new harmonic, rhythmic and notational systems continue to emerge.

Reinhold Glière (1875–1956)—p. 5
Sergei Prokofiev (1891–1953)—p. 19